Creative
SILK RIBBON
EMBROIDERY

Compiled by Gloria McKinnon

A J.B. Fairfax Press Publication

CONTENTS

EDITORIAL
Managing Editor: Judy Poulos
Editorial Assistant: Ella Martin
Editorial Coordinator: Margaret Kelly
Photography: Andrew Elton
Styling: Kathy Tripp
Illustrations: Lesley Griffith

DESIGN AND PRODUCTION
Manager: Anna Maguire
Design: Jenny Nossal
Cover Design: Jenny Pace
Production Editor: Sheridan Packer
Picture Editor: Cheryl Dubyk-Yates

Published by J.B. Fairfax Press Pty Limited
80-82 McLachlan Ave
Rushcutters Bay NSW, 2011 Australia
A.C.N. 003 738 430

Formatted by J.B. Fairfax Press Pty Limited

Printed by Toppan Printing Company,
Singapore
JBFP 464

CREATIVE SILK RIBBON EMBROIDERY
ISBN 1 86343 291 4

CONTENTS

INTRODUCTION

Embroidery is a way of life with me and has always been a large and important part of my life. I am very lucky to have had a mother and an aunt who both embroider beautifully and have always encouraged me. If talents are inherited, then my energy, love of flowers and embroidery are a legacy from my mother.

I grew up on a farm at Clunes where my mother did not know the meaning of the words, 'I'm bored' – you could always garden or stitch. I've never really liked digging in the soil (though I love the flowers), so it was stitching for me.

I love all styles of embroidery, but my favourites were needlepoint (we called it tapestry until we knew better) and crewel embroidery (which we referred to as fancywork). These eventually led me to silk ribbon embroidery which suits my life because it's quicker than needlepoint or crewel work, and it offers me a wide scope for developing new stitches. With silk ribbon, there are no set rules, leaving me free to experiment. If the result is pleasing, then that is how it was meant to be.

Over the years, I have taught many wonderful students in Australia, New Zealand and America. My American friend and heirloom sewing guru, Martha Pullen was teaching at my store, Anne's Glory Box, when she realised that silk ribbon embroidery would be the next big passion back home. She invited me to teach at the Martha Pullen school in Huntsville, Alabama, and I've been teaching there twice a year for the last eight years. Silk ribbon embroidery also suits my American students very well. They love the look of pretty embroidery but not the time it takes to complete. Silk ribbon embroidery grows so quickly – I tell them they will get instant gratification!

Many of my students have become my friends and it's just wonderful to see them developing their skills. I particularly love 'show and tell' when students bring their finished work. Seeing their pleasure is certainly part of the pleasure of teaching. The other great reward is to see someone develop from a non-embroiderer to a confident embroiderer.

It is important that these skills be taught to our daughters so they can share the gentle arts with their daughters. They will take the wonderful stitches we have developed and use them in a different way with a fresh eye, but the thread will be continuous through the years – a link of beautiful silk ribbon.

Silk ribbon is so versatile, it can be used on pillows, brooches, purses, garments, pictures for framing, pretty boxes, collars – or wherever takes your fancy.

My friend, Judith Montano teaches her beautiful crazy patchwork at my store. Many years ago, while on a visit here, Judith saw silk ribbon embroidery and was inspired by what she saw. She now incorporates her own style of silk ribbon embellishment into all that she does. Her book, *The Art of Silk Ribbon Embroidery*, is a best seller and profiles some Australian embroiderers. I am proud to be included.

I also give lectures on silk ribbon embroidery at stitches and craft shows around Australia, and it is interesting to see that there is still incredible interest and it still has a long way to go.

Embroidery is a great gift that links women of all ages. I find that I can still sit with my mother and sister and share the same feeling of togetherness as I did when my mother was teaching me. Wanting to share all of this has led me to compiling this book. I want to thank my husband, Don; my friend and store manager, Fay King, and Rob James and Judy Poulos from J.B. Fairfax Press for their support, patience and encouragement.

Gloria

GLORIA'S TIPS FOR SUCCESSFUL SILK RIBBON EMBROIDERY

I was first introduced to silk ribbon embroidery
by Melva McCameron, an Australian living in the
United States. It only took one day and I was hooked.

Working with silk ribbons is a very forgiving and rewarding form of embroidery: nature rarely forms a perfect flower, so you don't need to either. If you make a flower you are not entirely happy with, just keep going until the piece is completed, then judge if you need to redo the flower. Most times you will find you don't.

Silk ribbon embroidery is also rewarding: you see results immediately, because it covers so quickly.

RIBBONS

As a general rule, I use Kanagawa silk ribbons in widths from 2 to 7 mm ($^1/_{16}$ to $^5/_{16}$ in). Occasionally, I use an overdyed rayon ribbon.

I begin with a knot, others don't; there is no right or wrong way to do things – just different ways.

Any stitch that can be successfully done with wool or thread can be done with ribbon. The only difference is that you do not pull the ribbon as tightly as you do when working with thread.

Work with short lengths of ribbon. This page is a good length to use. When you begin, thread the ribbon

through the needle, then take the point of the needle back through the ribbon approximately 6 mm ($^1/_4$ in) from the end. This will allow you to use more of the ribbon (less waste) and save you searching around on the floor if the needle should fall.

Recently, gorgeous overdyed silk bias ribbons have become widely available. These ribbons can be used in the same way as the straight ribbons to create beautiful flowers. If the ribbon is being stitched through the fabric, take care to use only very short lengths. Bias ribbons work best for surface decoration where the flower is actually made in the hand, then attached to the fabric.

FABRIC

You can do silk ribbon embroidery on just about any fabric you can put a needle through. However, it is a good policy to buy the best fabric you can afford. It takes just as long to embroider a cheap fabric as a good one, but the result will be very different.

If you are making a piece that will need to be washed, take that into account when choosing your fabric.

NEEDLES

I like to use Piecemakers tapestry needles in sizes 20-26. The higher the number, the finer the needle.

EMBROIDERY HOOPS

I always use a small hoop because I find it comfortable to do so and it keeps my work even. Other people do lovely work without a hoop, so it's a matter of personal choice.

EMBROIDERY DESIGNS

Embroidery stitch books and stitch guides all have wonderful stitches just waiting to be worked in ribbon. Vintage linens are also a great source when looking for design ideas. In my glory box days, it was called fancy-work, and the doilies, traycloths, tea cosies and tablecloths have an old-world charm that we can reproduce in ribbon for a nostalgia trip.

Flower books and gardening books are another source of embroidery designs, giving you colour and placement ideas. A group of French or colonial knots in purple colours, wider at the top and tapering to nothing will be wisteria – the same stitches wider at the bottom and the same design, tapering away to nothing at the top will be hyacinths. Remember, you are only creating the illusion of a flower; you are not out to win a horticultural award!

To transfer a design to fabric from an old piece of linen or from a pattern book, photocopy or trace the design first, then transfer it to your fabric. This can be done in a variety of ways:
• Tape the photocopy up on a window or on a light box, then place the fabric over it and trace with a soft pencil.
• Using tissue paper, trace the design from the photocopy with a transfer pencil. Lay the tissue paper with the pencilled side down and iron the design onto the fabric. This will be permanent, but it will be a mirror image of the original.
• Place tulle or netting over the photocopy and trace the design using a biro or pen. Next, place the tulle or netting onto the fabric and, with a water-soluble pen or dixon pencil, draw over the lines. This will give you a series of dots with which to work.

DREAM BAG

Stitched by Lani Savage

Fill this lovely little bag with chamomile and lavender to lull you to sleep,
or make it for a little bridesmaid to scatter rosebuds from as she goes.

MATERIALS

2.5 m (2³/₄ yd) of 1.5 cm (⁵/₈ in) wide
  wired graduated ribbon,
  Pink to Green
2 m (2¹/₄ yd) of 2.5 cm (1 in) wide
  satin-edged organza ribbon, Ivory
2 m (2¹/₄ yd) of 2.5 cm (1 in) wide
  wired ribbon, Deep Pink to Green
2 m (2¹/₄ yd) of 5 cm (2 in) wide
  organza ribbon, Pink
2 m (2¹/₄ yd) of 4 mm (³/₁₆ in) wide
  silk ribbon: Mauve, Mushroom
1 m (1¹/₈ yd) each of 7 mm (⁵/₁₆ in)
  wide silk ribbon: Green, Cream,
  Mid-pink, Rose, Pale Mauve
25 cm (10 in) of ivory cotton damask
20 cm (8 in) each of wired ribbon in
  two shades of Green
Water-soluble marker pen
Lace pins
Cotton thread in a colour to blend
  with the ribbons
Tracing paper
Pencil

PREPARATION

See the pattern and the embroidery
design on pages 11 and 12.

STEP ONE

Cut four pieces of fabric, each 25 cm
(10 in) square.

STEP TWO

Lay ten pieces of 1.5 cm (⁵/₈ in) wide
Pink to Green wired ribbon across one
piece of fabric so that they just touch
one another (Fig. 1). Baste the ribbon
ends to the fabric.

STEP THREE

Weave the satin-edged organza
ribbon through the strips of ribbon
basted to the fabric. Baste the top
and bottom edges again to secure the
ribbons in place.

STEP FOUR

Trace the heart pattern and cut it out.
Centre the heart over the woven
ribbons and mark the outline in dots
with the water-soluble marker.

STEP FIVE

Layer two strands of silk ribbon: 4 mm
(³/₁₆ in) wide Mauve and 7 mm wide
Green. Starting at the dip in the heart,
twist the ribbons around the outline
of the heart, pinning them into position
as you go.

EMBROIDERY

STEP ONE

From the 7 mm (⁵/₁₆ in) wide silk ribbons, make sixteen concertina roses,
following figures 2-5; four Cream, four
Rose, three Pale Mauve and five Mid-
pink. Stitch these roses into position as
shown on the embroidery diagram.
The same stitches will also hold the
ribbons encircling the heart in place.

STEP TWO

Stitch the violets in ribbon stitch,
working five petals with a Cream
French knot centre. Stitch the leaves of
the violets in Mushroom.

STEP THREE

For the green leaves, cut out tiny
heart shapes from the Green ribbons
and stitch them on with one stitch,
as required. You may like to embroider a stem stitch line to trail the
leaves along.

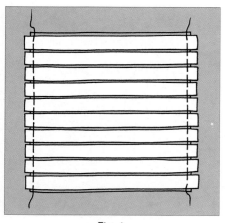

Fig. 1

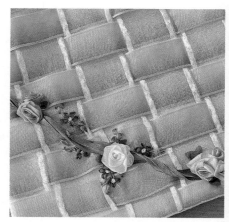

Silk ribbons used with wonderful variety

MAKING UP

STEP ONE

Place a second piece of fabric on the piece with the ribbons, with the right sides together. Stitch them together down two sides and across the base, leaving the top open. Turn the bag to the right side.

STEP TWO

Stitch the other two pieces of fabric together with the right sides facing, stitching the sides and base, leaving a 10 cm (4 in) opening in one side.

STEP THREE

Push the bag gently into the lining so the right sides are facing. Stitch around the top edge, making sure that all the ribbon ends are caught in the seams.

STEP FOUR

Turn the bag right side out by pulling the whole bag through the opening in the lining. Push the lining into the bag so that the corners are together.

STEP FIVE

Cut off 50 cm (20 in) of both the organza ribbon and the Deep Pink to Green wired ribbon and set them aside.

STEP SIX

Gather together the remaining organza and wired ribbons. Slip stitch them together to form a frill at the top of the bag, attaching the frill to the lining.

STEP SEVEN

Twist together the two remaining ribbons and tie a knot 2.5 cm (1 in) from each end. Attach the ribbons to the sides of the bag, 2.5 cm (1 in) from the top edge.

CONCERTINA ROSE

Thread a tapestry needle with a thread to match the ribbon and knot the end. Fold the ribbon at a right angle in the centre (Fig. 2).

Fold the horizontal part of the ribbon over and to the left. Bring the ribbon up from the bottom and fold it up and over. Fold the ribbon over from the left to the right and from the top down. Keep folding in this way until all the ribbon is used up (Figs 3, 4 and 5).

Grasp the two ends in one hand, then pull down gently on one of them (it doesn't matter which one) until a rose-shape is formed.

With the knotted thread, stitch down through the top and up again two or three times, finishing on the bottom. Wrap the base tightly with the thread, then finish off, leaving a 15 cm (6 in) tail of thread.

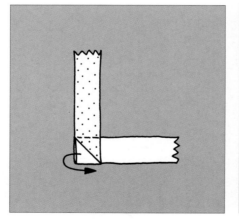

Fig. 2

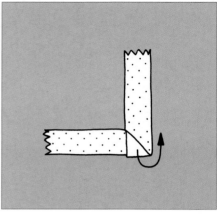

Fig. 3

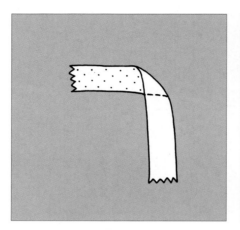

Fig. 4

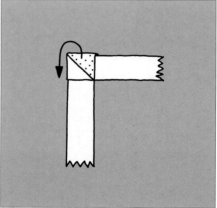

Fig. 5

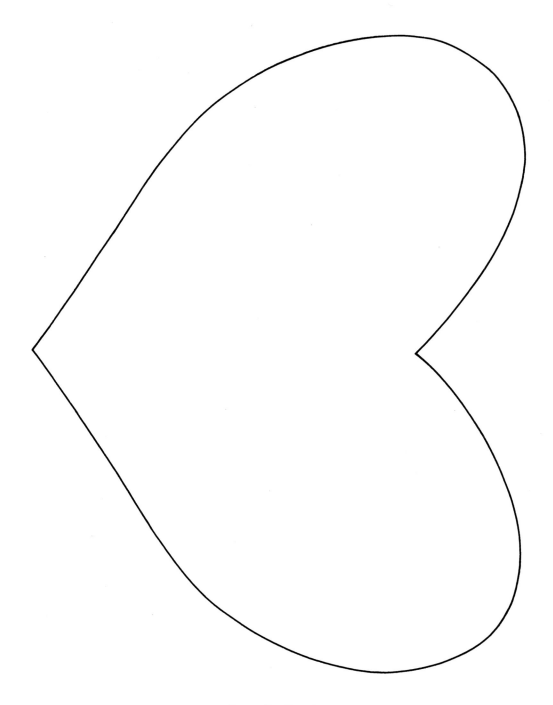

Dream Bag Template

Embroidery Design

ROSE PILLOW

Stitched by Fay King

Fabulous silk bias ribbon roses in delicate shades to complement the fabric, adorn this pretty segmented pillow.

MATERIALS

1 m (1¹/₈ yd) of self-embossed damask
Polyester fibre fill
1.5 m (1²/₃ yd) of 3.5 cm (1¹/₂ in) wide overdyed silk bias ribbon for each flower
1 m (1¹/₈ yd) of 15 mm (⁵/₈ in) wide overdyed silk ribbon, Green
Cotton thread to match the ribbons
Crewel needle, size 9
Gold cord
Doll needle, 18 cm (7 in) long
2.5 cm (1 in) self-cover button with shank

PREPARATION

PILLOW

Note: 6 mm (¹/₄ in) seams used.

STEP ONE

From the pillow fabric, cut two circles of fabric 30 cm (12 in) in diameter and one strip 8 cm x 92 cm (3 in x 36 in).

STEP TWO

Pin the strip around the circle and mark the seam line at the ends. Stitch the strip into a loop at the marks, then stitch one side of the loop to one of the circles. Pin the second circle to the other side of the loop and stitch it in place, leaving a 10 cm (4 in) opening. Turn the cover to the right side. Fill the cover very firmly, then close the opening with ladder stitch.

STEP THREE

Using a long length of cord in the doll needle, and beginning in the centre, make a loop around the pillow. Pull the cord up firmly to indent the pillow, then stitch around the pillow again. Repeat this to divide the pillow evenly into five sections (Fig. 1).

STEP FOUR

Cover the button with the pillow fabric, following the manufacturer's instructions and secure it at the centre of the pillow on one side.

EMBROIDERY

RIBBON ROSES

STEP ONE

Cut a 3.5 cm (1¹/₂ in) square of ribbon. Sew a circle of running stitches, then gather it up. Pull up the thread tightly and wrap it around the base. This will make the centre of the rose.

Lavish roses in graduated ribbon adorn this dainty pillow

STEP TWO

Fold 18 cm (7 in) of ribbon in half lengthwise. Using running stitches, stitch three petals along the ribbon (Fig. 2). Each petal will take approximately 5.5 cm (2¼ in) of ribbon. Pull up the thread to gather the petals, then take two back stitches to secure the thread (Fig. 3). Using the same thread, stitch the three petals around the flower centre.

STEP THREE

Cut 28 cm (11 in) of ribbon, fold and stitch five petals and attach them around the rose.

STEP FOUR

Cut 42 cm (16½ in) of ribbon, fold and stitch seven petals and attach them as before.

STEP FIVE

For the outer round of petals, cut 50 cm (20 in) of ribbon. Do not fold it, but stitch five petals, each 10 cm (4 in) long. Pull up the threads to gather the petals, then attach them as before. Make three roses, following steps one to five.

LEAVES

Fold 10 cm (4 in) of Green ribbon in half. Sew running stitches as shown in figure 4. Pull up the thread gently. When it is slightly gathered, end off with several small back stitches. Open out the leaf and set it aside. Make five to seven leaves.

MAKING UP

Arrange the flowers and leaves on the centre of the pillow. When you are pleased with the arrangement, stitch them into position.

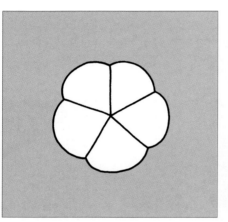

Fig. 1

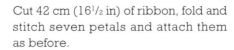

Fig. 2

Fig. 3

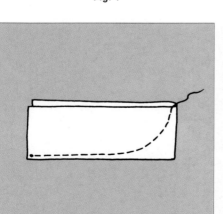

Fig. 4

Fig. 5

EMBROIDERED HAIRBAND

Stitched by Gloria McKinnon

What a pretty ornament for a little girl to wear for a special occasion!
Match the ribbon roses to the colours in her dress.

MATERIALS

Purchased velvet hairband
3 m (3¾ yd) each of Petals 7 mm
(⁵/₁₆ in) wide silk ribbon in two
shades of Pink
Silk threads: Burgundy, Pink, Green
Tapestry needle, size 22

EMBROIDERY

STEP ONE

Make nine twisted ribbon roses in Pale
Pink and seven roses in Dusty Pink. To
make a twisted rose, fold down one
end of the ribbon and lay the pin into
position as shown (Fig. 1).

STEP TWO

Roll the ribbon around the pin several
times to form the centre of the rose.
Thread the needle with the appropriate
coloured silk thread. Take a few
stitches through the base with the silk
thread to secure the centre of the rose.

STEP THREE

Fold the ribbon back and continue to
wind the rose in the same direction. As
you pass the folded section, stitch
through the base again, then make
another fold (Fig. 2). Keep folding,
winding and stitching until the rose
is the desired size, then wrap the
thread firmly around the base to
secure it. Leave a long length of thread
to attach the rose to the hairband.

MAKING UP

Attach the roses to the hairband, working outwards from the centre. Add
small lazy daisy stitch leaves in Green
silk thread and French knots in Burgundy and Pink.

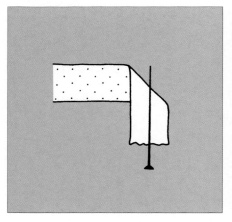

Fig. 1

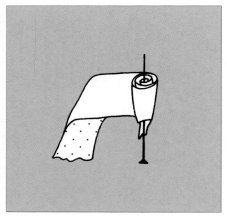

Fig. 2

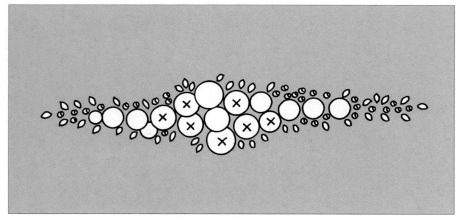

Embroidery Design

LAMP GARLAND

Stitched by Margaret B. Woolfe

Create instant romance with this lovely garland of silk flowers around the waist of a pretty purchased lampshade.

MATERIALS

30 cm (12 in) square of buckram

5.5 m (6 yd) of 4 cm (1¹/₂ in) wide ribbon, Cream with Gold edges

2 m (2¹/₄ yd) of 2.5 cm (1 in) wide wired ribbon, Rich Cream

1.5 m (1²/₃ yd) of 2.5 cm (1 in) wide wired ribbon, Grey to Blue

1 m (1¹/₈ yd) of 2.5 cm (1 in) wide organza ribbon: Gold, Gold-Black

1 m (1¹/₈ yd) of 4 mm (¹/₈ in) wide ribbon, Gold

2-3 sets of stamens

Craft glue

Needle

Neutral thread

Purchased lampshade, approximately 15 cm (6 in) diameter at the waist

Tracing paper

Pencil

Small amount of polyester fibre fill

PREPARATION

See the pattern on page 21.

STEP ONE

Trace the pattern. Make sure the pattern shape fits nicely around the lampshade. If adjustments need to be made, make the same adjustments to related measurements. Using the pattern, cut out one buckram shape.

STEP TWO

Cut two 1.6 m (1³/₄ yd) lengths of the Gold-edged Cream ribbon. With both pieces of the ribbon together, sew a gathering thread along the centre 40 cm (16 in) of the ribbon. Pull this over the buckram and pull up the gathering slightly to fit. Stitch the threads across each end of the buckram to secure the gathering.

MAKING THE FLOWERS

STEP ONE

Make two wound roses from the Gold-edged Cream ribbon, following figures 1-7 on pages 45 and 46.

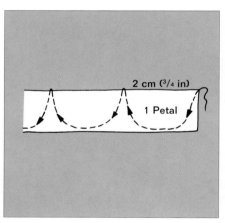

Fig. 1

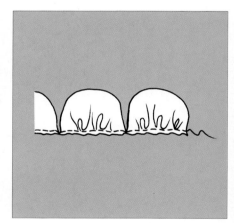

Fig. 2

Fig. 3

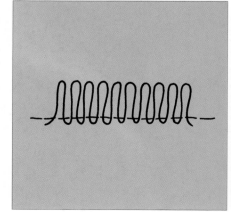

Fig. 4

STEP TWO

From the Gold-edged Cream ribbon, make one rose in the following way. Sew a gathering thread along the ribbon as shown in figure 1. Sew seven to nine petals. Pull up the gathering thread, then stitch the petals into a rose shape (Figs 2 and 3). For the centre, make approximately thirty 1 cm (³/₈ in) tall loops on a thread using the 6 mm (¹/₄ in) wide Gold ribbon (Fig. 4). Pull up on the thread and attach the loops at the centre of the rose.

Silver Accessories from Gwenda's Antiques, NSW; Silk Roses from Strattons, NSW; Dressing Table from Rustique, NSW

19

STEP THREE

Make two more wound roses in the Rich Cream wired ribbon in the same way as before. For the outer petals, cut five lengths of ribbon each 4 cm (1½ in) long. Gather them up with a running stitch, then pull up the thread (Figs 5 and 6). Attach the petals around the outer edge of the rose.

STEP FOUR

Make one flower with the puffed centre in Grey to Blue and one in Rich Cream. Cut 6.5 cm (2½ in) lengths of ribbon. Join the ends to form a loop. Gather the top and bottom edges with small running stitches. Pull up the gathering tightly to make a puff and tie off. Fill the puff with a small amount of fibre fill. Make five petals for the edge as for the first wound rose and attach them around the centre.

STEP FIVE

Cut 10 cm (4 in) of the Rich Cream ribbon. Sew the ends together to form a loop. For the rose centre, sew a gathering thread close to one edge and another 6 mm (¼ in) from the other edge, using slightly larger stitches. Pull up the close edge tightly and end off. Pull the other edge more loosely and end off. Glue a set of stamens into the cupola created. Make five petals as for the flower with the puffed centre and attach them around the edge.

STEP SIX

Make two or three wound roses from the Gold ribbons.

STEP SEVEN

Make the leaves from the 2.5 cm (1 in) wide Gold organza ribbon. Cut 8 cm (3 in) of ribbon and fold it in half to be 4 cm (1½ in). Stitch it as shown in figure 7. Open out the leaf and fold back the mitre. Gather it slightly at the end before attaching it. Make five to seven leaves.

MAKING UP

Attach the leaves first, then the flowers to the gathered band. Secure the band around the lampshade with a wonderful bow.

The monochromatic colour scheme is very elegant

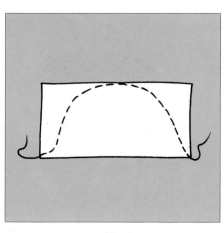

Fig. 5

Fig. 6

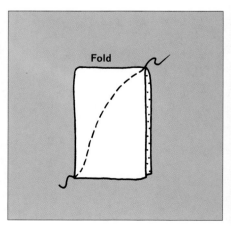

Fold

Fig. 7

20

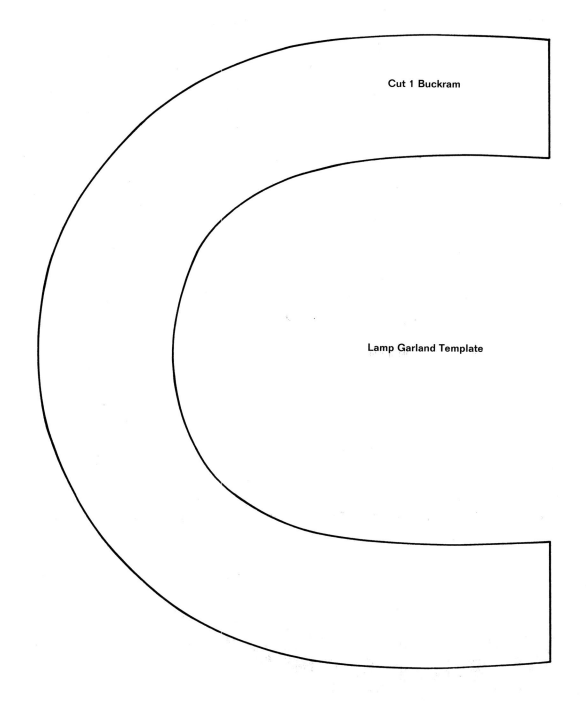

Cut 1 Buckram

Lamp Garland Template

PUFFING PILLOW

Stitched by Kathy Awender

Delightfully combining the heirloom sewing technique of puffing with silk ribbon embroidery, this pillow is a little charmer.

Finished size: approximately 25 cm x 35.5 cm (10 in x 14 in) plus the ruffle

MATERIALS

80 cm (⁷⁄₈ yd) of white Swiss batiste
1.4 m (1¹⁄₂ yd) of 12 mm (¹⁄₂ in) wide insertion lace
1.2 m (1¹⁄₄ yd) of 1.5 cm (⁵⁄₈ in) wide lace edging
2.3 m (2¹⁄₂ yd) of entredeux
Fine machine sewing thread
Two pieces of fabric, each 30 cm x 38 cm (12 in x 15 in)
4 m (4¹⁄₂ yd) of 32 mm (1¹⁄₄ in) wide silk ribbon, Pale Pink
1.85 m (2 yd) of 7 mm (⁵⁄₁₆ in) wide silk ribbon, Pale Pink
1.85 m (2 yd) each of 4 mm (³⁄₁₆ in) wide silk ribbon: Pale Pink, Pale Green, White
Stranded cotton, Pale Green
Water-soluble marker pen
Embroidery hoop
Ordinary sewing thread

EMBROIDERY

PILLOW TOP

See the embroidery design on page 24.

STEP ONE

Mark a strip of Swiss batiste 7.5 cm x 30 cm (3 in x 12 in), but do not cut it out until after the embroidery has been completed. Using the water-soluble marker pen, lightly trace the embroidery design onto the centre of this panel.

STEP TWO

Work the embroidery following the diagram and the key.

STEP THREE

To make silk ribbon puffing strips, cut two strips of 32 mm (1¹⁄₄ in) wide silk ribbon, each 50 cm (20 in) long. Gather each side of both strips to 30 cm (12 in). **Hint:** Practise on a small scrap of ribbon. Have the machine setting L=1.8 and W=2. Lay ordinary sewing thread along the ribbon edge and zigzag over it. Hold the tails of the thread to start. Work on the edge of the silk ribbon, but don't allow the edge to roll as you zigzag. Start and end 6-12 mm (¹⁄₄-¹⁄₂ in) from the ends of the ribbon. Do the first few stitches turning the flywheel by hand.

STEP FOUR

Sew a piece of entredeux to both long sides of the lace insertion. Sew a strip of lace with entredeux to each side of both puffing strips.

Dainty embroidery complements the puffing

STEP FIVE

For the side panels, pull a thread to straighten the fabric, then cut two strips, each 12 cm x 30 cm (5 in x 12 in). On each strip, pull a thread 3 cm (1¹⁄₄ in) from one long edge. Crease the strip on the pulled thread line and sew a 6 mm (¹⁄₄ in) tuck. Beginning 7.5 cm (3 in) from the end, pinch in every 5 cm (2 in) by sewing across the fold. Pull the thread snugly and knot it to secure. Work one French knot with 7 mm (⁵⁄₁₆ in) Pale Pink and two leaves with the 4 mm (³⁄₁₆ in) wide Pale Green at each pinch.

STEP SIX

Pull a thread 2.5 cm (1 in) from the fold of the tuck to make a placement line for the gathered edging. Cut the lace edging into two equal pieces and gather them to fit the length of the tucked side panels. Sew the edging in place along the pulled thread with a zigzag or pin stitch.

STEP SEVEN

Sew a puffing and insertion lace strip to each side of the embroidered centre panel. Add the side panels.

STEP EIGHT

Trace the outer edges of the pillow top, it should be approximately 25 cm x 35 cm (10 in x 14 in), being careful to centre the embroidery. Cut out the piece 12 mm (¹⁄₂ in) from the traced line for a seam allowance.

PILLOW BACK

Cut two pieces of Swiss batiste 30 cm x 46 cm (12 in x 18 in) for the pillow back. Fold them in half to make two 30 cm x 23 cm (12 in x 9 in) rectangles. Overlap the folded edges for 5 cm (2 in) and baste them together. Trim the joined piece to match the size of the pillow top.

RUFFLE

Cut two strips of Swiss batiste, each 10 cm x 137 cm (4 in x 54 in). Seam the short ends together to form a loop. Press the loop over double. Cut the 32 mm (1¼ in) wide silk ribbon the same length as the fabric ruffle. Seam the short ends, then baste the ribbon over the fabric ruffle, lining up the cut edge of the fabric with one edge of the ribbon. Gather along the long cut edge. Baste the ruffle to the pillow top with the right sides facing, spacing the gathers evenly.

MAKING UP

With the right sides facing, sew the pillow top to the back, sandwiching the ruffle in between. Trim the seam allowance to 6 mm (¼ in). Zigzag to finish the raw edges. Turn the pillow right side out.

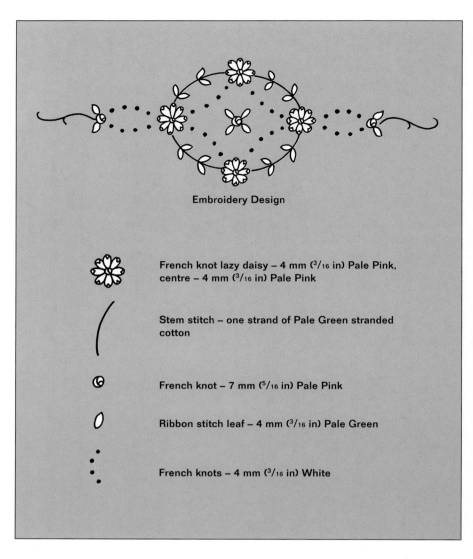

Embroidery Design

French knot lazy daisy – 4 mm (³/₁₆ in) Pale Pink, centre – 4 mm (³/₁₆ in) Pale Pink

Stem stitch – one strand of Pale Green stranded cotton

French knot – 7 mm (⁵/₁₆ in) Pale Pink

Ribbon stitch leaf – 4 mm (³/₁₆ in) Pale Green

French knots – 4 mm (³/₁₆ in) White

VICTORIAN BRIDE

Made by Judith Coombe from Judith and Kathryn Designs

Our beautiful bride wears a veil of old Maltese lace
and carries a bouquet of embroidered silk flowers.

MATERIALS

Preprinted silk panel
20 cm (8 in) of cream satin
Ordinary sewing thread, Cream
Variety of laces in cream and
  deep mauve
Variety of beads: gold, blue, clear,
  pearl
1 m (1 1/8 yd) of 12 mm (1/2 in)
  overdyed silk bias ribbon: Pale
  Pink, Pink to Green
1.5 m (1 2/3 yd) of 7 mm (5/16 in) wide
  satin ribbon, Cream
30 cm (12 in) of 4 mm (3/16 in) wide
  satin ribbon, Green
Six glass flower beads
Nymo thread
Straw, milliner's needle or beading
  needle, size 9
Polyester fibre fill

PREPARATION

STEP ONE

With right sides facing, stitch the front
and the back together, leaving a 10 cm
(4 in) opening at the base. It is best
to use a small stitch on your sewing
machine for this – it will help to keep
the edges smooth. Clip the curves and
turn the doll to the right side.

STEP TWO

Lightly and evenly stuff the doll with the
fibre fill, then slipstitch the opening
closed.

EMBROIDERY

STEP ONE

Make two rolled roses from the Pink to
Green silk bias ribbon and four rolled
roses from the Cream satin ribbon.
Beside each satin ribbon rose, attach a
small folded leaf made from the Green
satin ribbon.

STEP TWO

Make one Pale Pink rose by running a
gathering thread along the edge of the
ribbon approximately 3 mm (1/8 in)
from the edges. Start the rose with a
small tight roll, then gently roll the rest
of the gathered ribbon to create a rose.
Stitch through the base to secure.

STEP THREE

Arrange the ribbon roses and glass
flower beads to create the bouquet.
Stitch the flowers to the doll. Thread
several lengths of beads and pearls,
between 2.5 cm (1 in) and 4 cm (1 1/2 in)
long, onto the Nymo thread. Attach the
lengths of beads under the bouquet.

STEP FOUR

Stitch small motifs cut from the laces
around the flowers and trailing up
to the doll's shoulders. Attach the
gathered rose at the right shoulder.

STEP FIVE

Arrange the cream lace veil from the
back of the head and stitch it into
position. Arrange the deep mauve
lace over the top of the cream lace and
stitch it into position.

STEP SIX

Stitch a few beads scattered across the
doll's bodice.

SILK LAVENDER SACHETS

Stitched by Gloria McKinnon

Be ready for the gift-giving season with these delightful embroidered sachets, featuring some special silk ribbons.

MATERIALS

For all the sachets
15 cm x 76 cm (6 in x 30 in) of dupion silk
1 m (1¹⁄₈ yd) of ribbon for the neck
Small embroidery hoop
Lavender

For the pansy sachet
1 m (1¹⁄₈ yd) each of four colours of 7 mm (⁵⁄₁₆ in) wide silk ribbon (overdyed ribbons are very suitable)
2 m (2¹⁄₄ yd) of 4 mm (³⁄₁₆ in) wide silk ribbon, Dark Green
2 m (2¹⁄₄ yd) of 4 mm (³⁄₁₆ in) wide overdyed silk ribbon, Pale Pink
1 m (1¹⁄₈ yd) of 4 mm (³⁄₁₆ in) wide silk ribbon, Black or a dark contrasting colour
1 m (1¹⁄₈ yd) of 4 mm (³⁄₁₆ in) wide silk ribbon, Yellow
DMC Stranded Cotton, Dark Green
Piecemakers tapestry needle, size 22
Piecemakers crewel needle, size 9

For the rose bowl
10 m (11 yd) each of 4 mm (³⁄₁₆ in) wide ribbon: overdyed Pink to Lemon, Pink, Pale Pink
4 m (4¹⁄₂ yd) of 4 mm (³⁄₁₆ in) wide silk ribbon, Peach
8 m (9 yd) of 2 mm (¹⁄₁₆ in) wide silk ribbon, White
8 m (9 yd) of 4 mm (³⁄₁₆ in) wide overdyed ribbon, Beige to Green

DMC Stranded Cotton: Pale Green, Light Tan
Piecemakers tapestry needle, size 22
Piecemakers crewel needle, size 9

For the Canterbury bells
5 m (5¹⁄₂ yd) each of 4 mm (³⁄₁₆ in) wide silk ribbon: two shades of Cream, four shades of Mauve
1 m (1¹⁄₈ yd) of 4 mm (³⁄₁₆ in) wide silk ribbon: Plum, Green
DMC Stranded Cotton, Dark Green
Piecemakers tapestry needle, size 22
Piecemakers crewel needle, size 9

For the impatiens spray
3 m (3¹⁄₃ yd) of 7 mm (⁵⁄₁₆ in) wide silk ribbon, Pink
5 m (5¹⁄₂ yd) of 4 mm (³⁄₁₆ in) wide silk ribbon: Pale Pink, White, Pale Blue
2 m (2¹⁄₄ yd) of 4 mm (³⁄₁₆ in) wide silk ribbon, Yellow
DMC Stranded Cotton, Grey/Green
Piecemakers tapestry needle, size 22
Piecemakers crewel needle, size 9

PREPARATION

ALL FOUR SACHETS

See the four embroidery designs on pages 30 to 31.

STEP ONE

Overlock or zigzag the edges of the silk as it frays very quickly. Fold the dupion silk in half to mark the base line of the sachet.

STEP TWO

Secure the fabric in the embroidery hoop. Following the stitch guide, commence the embroidery the distance above the base line indicated for each sachet: Canterbury bells, 2.5 cm (1 in); impatiens spray, 4.5 cm (1³⁄₄ in); pansy, 3 cm (1¹⁄₄ in); rose bowl, 1.5 cm (⁵⁄₈ in).

EMBROIDERY

Embroider each of the flower designs following the diagrams and the stitch guide.

MAKING UP

When the embroidery is completed, fold the sachet over double with the right sides together. Stitch down the sides. Turn the sachet through to the right side, taking care to push the corners right out. Fold the top of the sachet right in until it reaches the base line. Fill your sachet with lavender, then tie a beautiful bow around the neck.

STITCH GUIDE

PANSY SACHET

PANSIES

Using 7 mm ($^5/_{16}$ in) wide silk ribbon in the tapestry needle, make six straight stitch petals as shown.

Using the Black or a dark contrasting coloured silk ribbon, make four small straight stitches.

DAISIES

Make five petals in ribbon stitch with a Yellow French knot centre.
Leaves are lazy daisy stitch.
Buds are straight stitches in silk ribbon with an open fly stitch in a single strand of Dark Green cotton.
Stems are Dark Green stem stitch.

ROSE BOWL SACHET

Roses are worked in overdyed and silk ribbons in fly stitch.
Buds and leaves are ribbon stitch.
Fillers are French knots.
Bowl outline is in stem stitch, using one strand of Light Tan cotton.
Other stems and buds are in open fly stitch, using one strand of Pale Green.

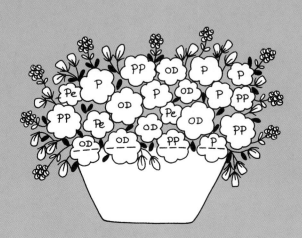

STITCH GUIDE

CANTERBURY BELLS SACHET

Canterbury bells are worked in ribbon stitch, starting from 6 mm (¹/₄ in) from the base of the stem and working up. Overlap the bottom three or four pairs as they get smaller. Work three French knots at the top.

Stems are stem stitch using a single strand of cotton.

Leaves are lazy daisy stitch using a single strand of Dark Green cotton.

Mini-delphiniums are French knots, tapering upwards, worked in four shades of Mauve.

Daisies are ribbon stitch with a French knot centre.

IMPATIENS SPRAY SACHET

This flower has five petals which sit out from the fabric.

Using the 7 mm (⁵/₁₆ in) wide ribbon, bring the needle up from the back then take it to the back, leaving a petal of approximately 8 mm (³/₈ in) standing free. Hold that petal in your fingers when working the next petal. Work the five petals in the order shown. The centre is a Yellow colonial knot.

Stems are stem stitch in one strand of Grey/Green cotton.

Other stitches used: Fly stitch roses, ribbon stitch buds, French knot forget-me-nots, colonial knot alyssum and lazy daisy leaves.

POPPY PILLOW

Stitched by Lyn Sylvester

These wonderful California poppies add another dimension to silk ribbon embroidery. The overdyed silk bias ribbon is soft and pliable and ideal for this project.

MATERIALS

1.2 m (1 1/3 yd) of silk fabric
3.5 m (3 3/4 yd) of 12 mm (1/2 in) wide
  overdyed silk bias ribbon or of
  12 mm (1/2 in) wide silk ribbon
Kanagawa silk twist thread, Light
  Olive Green
DMC Stranded Cotton to match the
  silk ribbon
Piecemakers crewel needle, size 9
23 cm x 30 cm (9 in x 12 in) of tulle
  or net
40 cm (16 in) square of Pellon
Waterproof laundry marker
Water-soluble marker pen
Polyester fibre fill

PREPARATION

See the embroidery design on page 35.

STEP ONE

Cut a 40 cm (16 in) square from the silk fabric. Because the silk frays so readily, it is a good idea to overlock or zigzag the edges.

Baste the Pellon to the back of the silk square.

STEP TWO

Trace the design onto the tulle or net using the laundry marker and allow it to dry completely.

STEP THREE

Centre the tracing over the square of silk and mark the design using the water-soluble marker pen. This will leave a series of dots on the fabric. **Note:** It is always advisable to test the water-soluble marker pen on a scrap of the fabric before you begin.

EMBROIDERY

STEP ONE

Complete the embroidery of the stems and leaves before working the flowers. Work the stems and leaf veins in stem stitch, using a small even stitch. Work the leaves in straight stitch, following the outlines to give the shape (Fig. 1). Use the Kanagawa silk twist thread for all the stems and leaves.

STEP TWO

For buds 1 and 2, cut approximately 12 mm (1/2 in) of silk ribbon and fold it in half lengthwise (Fig. 2). Fold the ribbon over to form a bud (Fig. 3) then, using one strand of cotton, sew a gathering thread across the base (Fig. 4). Pull up the thread to gather the ribbon, tie off the ends and fold the raw edges to the back. Appliqué the bud into position.

Fig. 1

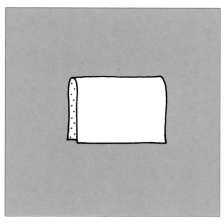

Fig. 2

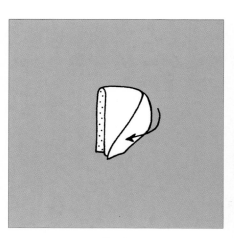

Fig. 3

STEP THREE

For bud 3, cut approximately 2.5 cm (1 in) of silk ribbon. Fold the ends to the back to make a loop (Fig. 5). Sew a gathering thread across the base. Pull up the thread to gather the ribbon and tie off the ends. Turn the ribbon through so that the gathering is on the inside. Stitch the bud into place. Fix the top of the bud in place with a tiny stitch.

STEP FOUR

For poppies 1 and 2, cut the remaining ribbon into three lengths. Using a single strand of cotton, sew a gathering thread along one long edge of the ribbon. As you form the poppies, ease the ribbon along this edge as you go. For the first petal, starting at point **A**, attach the ribbon to the fabric with a small stitch. To begin forming the poppy, fold back approximately 6 mm (¹/₄ in) of ribbon and stitch so that the ruffled edge lies along the line **A-B**. When you are approaching point **B**, cut off the ribbon and fold back approximately 6 mm (¹/₄ in) of ribbon as before. Stitch right to point **B**. Start the second petal just behind the first, bringing it around to finish at point **C** (beginning and ending with a fold as before). Now, make the third petal so that it comes in front of the first. Still using the one strand of cotton, catch the outer edges of these petals approximately 3 mm (¹/₈ in) from the outer edge at approximately 12 mm (1¹/₂ in) intervals, ensuring that each small stitch is hidden among the gathers. This will hold the petals onto the fabric. You will need to take one row of gathered ribbon across in front of these three petals starting at the base of the third petal and crossing to point **C**. When this row is in place, it is time to embroider the stamens in pistol stitch and French knots. Work the stamens onto the base of the last petal. Work the fourth petal in two parts. Attach a row of gathered ribbon, starting at point **D** and working back towards point **C** (with the frill lying across the stamens). Do not cut the ribbon off at this point, but work back towards point **D** with the frill lying away from the centre. When the petal is attached, turn it up toward the centre and catch it as before to hold it.

STEP FIVE

For poppy 3, work in the same way as for poppies 1 and 2, except that the fifth petal will lie away from the centre, then a sixth petal will lie towards the centre over the fifth one (as for the last petal on the other flowers). Follow the arrows on the pattern for the placement and direction of the petals.

MAKING UP

STEP ONE

Cut four 20 cm (8 in) wide strips across the width of the silk fabric. With the right sides together, stitch the ends together to make a loop. Fold the loop over double with the wrong sides together. Overlock or zigzag the raw edges together to reduce fraying. Mark the loop into quarters.

STEP TWO

Stitch two rows of gathering around the loop and pull up the ruffle to fit the pillow. Pin the ruffle to the pillow, matching the quarter marks to the corners, with the frill facing the centre and making sure that all the seams are hidden within the gathers. Stitch.

STEP THREE

Cut a 40 cm (16 in) square of silk for the back. Pin the pillow back and front together, with the right sides facing and the ruffle sandwiched in between. Stitch around three sides and 3 cm (1¹/₄ in) onto the fourth side at each end. Turn the pillow to the right side through the opening, making sure that the corners are square. Fill the pillow and slipstitch the opening closed.

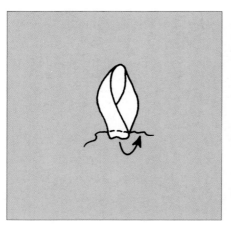

Fig. 4

Fig. 5

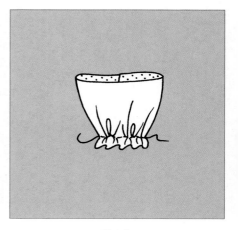

Fig. 6

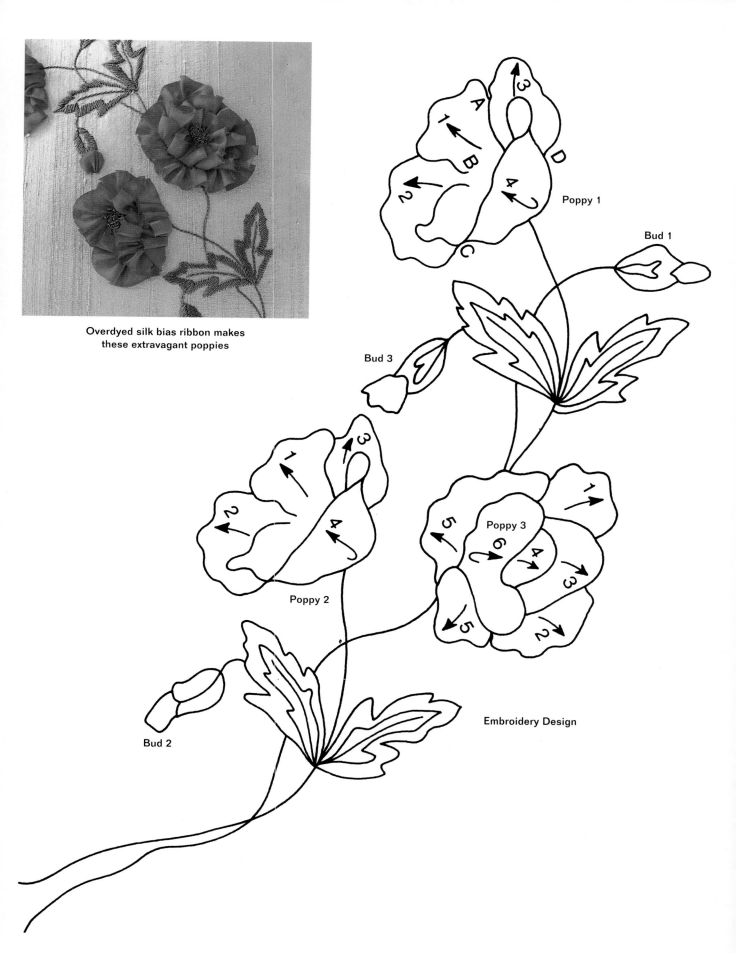

Overdyed silk bias ribbon makes
these extravagant poppies

Poppy 1

Bud 1

Bud 3

Poppy 2

Poppy 3

Embroidery Design

Bud 2

35

PHOTO ALBUM

Stitched by Jan Bond for Judith and Kathryn Designs

Antiqued lace, beads and ribbon roses make this masterpiece photo album which would be a treasure to keep or to give as a gift.

MATERIALS

Photo album that can be taken apart
1 m (1¹⁄₈ yd) of black silk fabric
Printed silk picture
Various lace motifs
2 m (2¹⁄₄ yd) of fine gold cord
Embroidery thread, Gold
Antique glass seed beads, mixed blues
Small gold beads
1 m (1¹⁄₈ yd) each of 7 mm (⁵⁄₁₆ in) wide silk ribbon: Pink, Deep Pink
2 m (2¹⁄₄ yd) of 4 mm (³⁄₁₆ in) wide silk ribbon, Green (or the same length in total of two or three greens)
1 m (1¹⁄₈ yd) each of 7 mm (⁵⁄₁₆ in) wide organza ribbon: Deep Pink, Red
Lightweight wadding
Cardboard for mounting
Craft glue
Nymo thread
Piecemakers tapestry needle, size 22
Straw needle, size 9
Embroidery needle, size 8
Embroidery hoop, 15 cm (6 in)

EMBROIDERY

STEP ONE

Thread the tapestry needle with both the silk ribbon and the organza ribbon together. Place the silk panel in the embroidery hoop and embroider over the roses in ribbon stitch (Fig. 1).

STEP TWO

Embroider several buds in the picture with the Pink silk ribbon and the Red organza ribbon in the needle together. Work a small Green ribbon stitch at the base of the bud. Work Green ribbon stitches over the leaves around the border.

STEP THREE

The embellishing trails are stitched in Gold thread in wheat stitch. This is worked as a lazy daisy stitch with a second straight stitch (Fig. 2). Work the stitches in line to create a chain.

STEP FOUR

Attach large groups of the beads, using the straw needle and the Nymo thread.

MAKING UP

STEP ONE

Cut a piece of the wadding to the size of the picture. Baste it to the back of the work. Cut a piece of cardboard to the size of the finished piece. Glue the edges of the silk fabric over onto the back of the cardboard.

STEP TWO

Cut a square of wadding the size of the album cover. Cut out a piece from it the same size as the silk picture. Cover the album with the black silk, then glue the picture into the area where the wadding has been removed.

STEP THREE

Glue gold cord around the picture and around the outer edge. Position the lace motifs, then glue them into place. Add extra beads where needed.

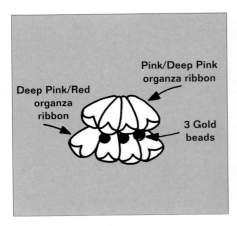

Fig. 1

Variety is the key to this design

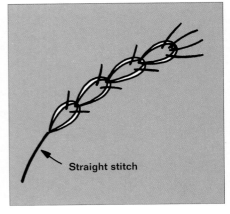

Straight stitch

Fig. 2

PANSY PILLOW

Stitched by Gloria McKinnon

This charming little pillow combines delicate lace and silk ribbon embroidery to produce a unique effect. The pansies are slightly tricky to perfect, so take a little time to practise before you begin working on the lace.

MATERIALS

Two pieces of moiré fabric, each
  25 cm x 30 cm (10 in x 12 in)
Two 20 cm (8 in) wide strips of moiré
  fabric, cut across the full width of
  the fabric, for the ruffle
30 cm (12 in) of 12 cm (4¹⁄₂ in)
  wide lace
4 m (4¹⁄₂ yd) each of 4 mm (³⁄₁₆ in)
  wide silk ribbon: Lemon Yellow,
  Blue/green, Pale Blue, Olive Green
2 m (2¹⁄₄ yd) each of 4 mm (³⁄₁₆ in)
  wide silk ribbon: Yellow, Black,
  Pink
Kanagawa silk twist thread, Olive
  Green
Embroidery thread, Blue/Green
10 m (11 yd) of 4 mm (³⁄₁₆ in) wide
  silk ribbon, Pale Pink
Assortment of Piecemakers tapestry
  needles, sizes 20-24
1 m (1¹⁄₈ yd) of piping cord
2.5 cm x 1 m (1 in x 1¹⁄₈ yd) of fabric
  for the piping
Matching sewing thread
Polyester fibre fill

PREPARATION

See the embroidery design and key on page 41.

Baste the lace across the centre of one piece of the moiré fabric, matching centre lines.

EMBROIDERY

Following the embroidery design and the stitch guide, embroider the pansies and other flowers as shown, taking the stitches through the lace and the moiré fabric. This is a little harder than the usual silk ribbon embroidery, but persevere – it will be worth it.

MAKING UP

STEP ONE

Fold the piping fabric over double with the wrong sides together. Place the piping cord inside the folded fabric. Using the zipper foot on your sewing machine, stitch along the piping, as close as possible to the cord. Pin the piping around the right side of the embroidered piece, with the raw edges even. Clip the seam allowance of the piping to allow it to curve around the corners. Trim the ends of the piping so that one end overlaps the other end for 2.5 cm (1 in). Undo the stitching for 2.5 cm (1 in) on the longer end and cut out the cord for this length. Turn a small hem on the longer end of the fabric. Lay the shorter end of the piping inside the hemmed end. Using the zipper foot on your sewing machine, stitch around the pillow to secure the piping, stitching as close to the cord as you can.

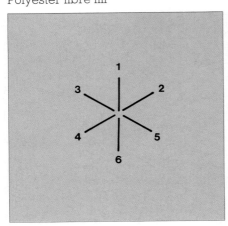

Fig. 1

Fig. 2

Fig. 3

STEP TWO

Join the two strips of ruffle fabric together to form a loop. Fold the loop over double, with the wrong sides together and the raw edges even. Divide the length of the loop into quarters and mark these points with pins. Sew two rows of gathering stitches along the raw edge of the ruffle. Pull up the gathering to fit around the pillow. Pin the ruffle to the right side of the pillow front, placing a pin at each corner. Adjust the gathering, then stitch on the wrong side following the piping stitching line.

STEP THREE

Place the pillow front on top of the pillow back with the ruffle pointing towards the centre of the pillow. Stitch around three sides and for 2.5 cm (1 in) on both ends of the fourth side, stitching along the same line as before. Clip across the corners and turn the pillow to the right side. Carefully stuff the pillow, taking care to push the stuffing right into the corners. Neatly slipstitch the opening closed.

Lifelike pansies, stitched through lace, are a delight

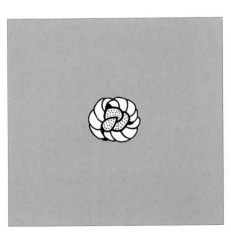

Fig. 4

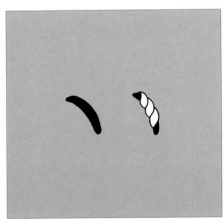

Fig. 5

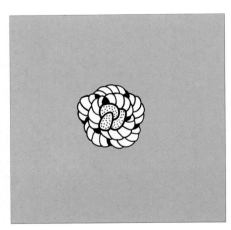

Fig. 6

Lilac pansies with Black straight stitch and Yellow French knot centres

Leaves in detached chain stitch

Lazy Daisy with French knot centre

Jenny Bradford's wrapped rose with French knot centre

Forget-me-not with 5 Blue French knots and Lemon French knot centre

Embroidery Design and Key

41

EMBELLISHED SWEATER

Stitched by Gloria McKinnon

Beautiful to look at and delightful to wear, this glamorous addition to your wardrobe is quite simple to make.

MATERIALS

Purchased sweater
1 m (1 1/8 yd) each of 12 mm (1/2 in) wide rayon ribbon: Burgundy, Deep Green, Old Gold
2 m (2 1/4 yd) each of 4 mm (3/16 in) wide silk ribbon: Purple, Cream
Silk thread, Gold
Piecemakers tapestry needle, size 22

PREPARATION

See the embroidery design below.

Divide the front neck of the sweater for the seven major flowers as indicated in figure 1. There are three burgundy flowers, marked **O** (one in the centre and two others). The flowers marked **X** are Old Gold.

EMBROIDERY

STEP ONE

Stitch the seven major flowers first, then the leaves, then the other flowers. For the major flowers, using ribbon stitch and making each petal 17 mm (3/4 in) long, make five petals. For ribbon stitch, pass the needle back through the centre of the ribbon and pull through gently to the back.

STEP TWO

With the Deep Green rayon ribbon, make three ribbon stitch leaves on each side of the flower. The Old Gold flowers have two leaves on the side away from the centre.

STEP THREE

In the centre of each flower, work three French knots using the silk thread.

STEP FOUR

Between each major flower, work two Purple flowers in lazy daisy stitch.

STEP FIVE

Fill all the spaces with baby's breath worked in French knots in the Cream 4 mm silk ribbon.

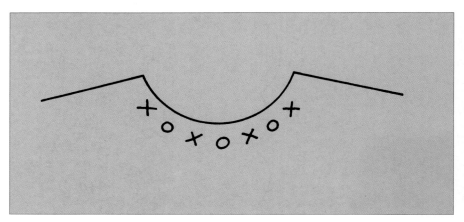

Fig. 1

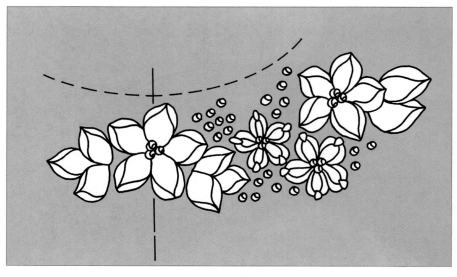

Embroidery Design

VASE OF ROSES

Stitched by Therese Turley

The vase made from bread dough is the feature of this pretty embroidered posy. These vases are readily available at craft and needlework shops in a variety of designs.

MATERIALS

25 cm (10 in) square of textured cotton or upholstery damask for the background

2 m (2¼ yd) of 12 mm (½ in) wide rayon ribbon, Mauve

1 m (1⅛ yd) of 7 mm (⁵/₁₆ in) wide silk ribbon, Plum

2 m (2¼ yd) of 3 mm (⅛ in) wide silk ribbon, Mauve

1 m (1⅛ yd) of 1 cm (⅜ in) wide organza ribbon, Green

40 cm (15¾ in) of 7 mm (⁵/₁₆ in) wide silk ribbon, Dusky Pink

Two thicknesses of Gold thread

Fifteen small glass beads, Copper

Beading needle

Piecemakers tapestry needle, size 22

Piecemakers crewel needle, size 9

Bread dough vase

Craft glue

Fray Check (optional)

Sewing threads to match the ribbons

PREPARATION

Overlock the edges of the fabric or treat them with the Fray Check.

Fold the fabric in half, then fold it into quarters to find the centre. Mark the centre point – this is where you will place the top of the vase.

MAKING ROSES

FLOWERS AND LEAVES

Note: It is best not to cut a separate length of ribbon for each rose, but to work with the whole length and cut each rose off as it is completed.

STEP ONE

Following figures 1 to 7, make eight small roses, using Mauve silk ribbon; four medium-sized roses, using Plum ribbon; and three large roses, using Mauve rayon ribbon.

Tiny roses massed in a vase for a striking display

STEP TWO

Make six buds, using 4 cm (1½ in) each of the Green organza ribbon and the Dusky Pink silk ribbon for each bud. To make a bud, lay the Dusky Pink ribbon on top of the Green ribbon and treat them as a single piece, varying the position of the Dusky Pink ribbon (up or down) to vary the growth of the bud. Lay one end of the ribbons over the other end, pinching them together to form the base of the bud. Pull the top up to a point. Secure the base of the bud by winding thread around it, then stitch through the base, ending with a knot.

STEP THREE

Make the leaves in the same way as the buds, but using only the Green ribbon.

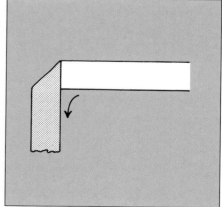

Fig. 1

MAKING UP

STEP ONE

Arrange all the roses, buds and leaves into an attractive bouquet, then stitch them onto the background fabric.

STEP TWO

Using the finer Gold thread, work three or four fly stitch leaves. Using the same Gold thread, sew on the glass beads in groups of three between the leaves.

STEP THREE

Using the thicker Gold thread, work random straight stitches, topped with a straight stitch in Mauve silk ribbon.

STEP FOUR

Glue on the bread dough vase. Frame the picture with a suitable frame.

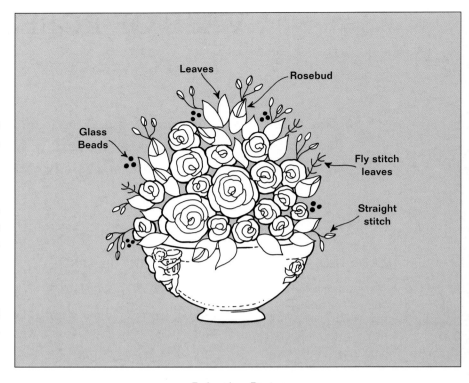

Embroidery Design

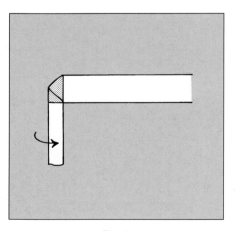

Fig. 2

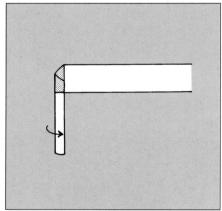

Fig. 3

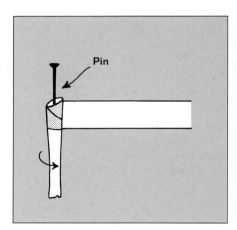

Fig. 4

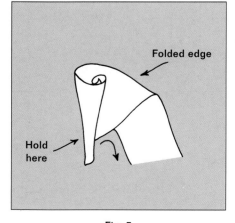

Fig. 5

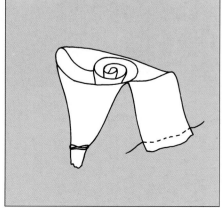

Fig. 6

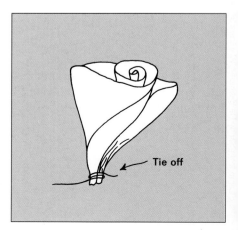

Fig. 7

Fabric and Lamp from Sandy De Beyer, NSW; Cards from Mosman Antiques, NSW; Vase and Powder Pot from Home and Garden on the Mall, NSW

47

SILK PILLOWS

Made by Gloria McKinnon

These sumptuous little pillows can be used for brooches, hat pins, sewing pins or just as a wonderful decoration on your dressing table.

MATERIALS

For each pillow

20 cm x 25 cm (8 in x 10 in) of dupion silk
Polyester fibre fill
Stuffing tool

For the roses and lace pillow

2 m (2¼ yd) each of 12 mm (½ in) wide overdyed silk bias ribbon: Pink to Green, Dusty Pink, Autumn Pink
50 cm (20 in) each of 12 mm (½ in) wide overdyed silk bias ribbon, two shades of Green
Two guipure lace motifs
Piecemakers crewel needle, size 9
Neutral sewing thread

For the rose spray pillow

Seven flocked rose leaves
2 m (2¼ yd) of 4 cm (1½ in) wide overdyed silk bias ribbon, Dusty Pink
1.5 m (1⅔ yd) of 4 mm (³⁄₁₆ in) wide silk ribbon, Pale Pink

For the buttons and lace pillow

50 cm (20 in) of 7.5 cm (3 in) wide cream guipure lace
1 m (1⅛ yd) of 4 cm (1½ in) wide vintage silk ribbon, Dusty Rose
50 cm (20 in) of 4 cm (1½ in) wide vintage silk ribbon, Green
Perle No. 5 thread, 739
Craft glue
'Antique' mother-of-pearl buttons in various sizes
Two brass hearts
1 m (1⅛ yd) of 4 mm (³⁄₁₆ in) wide silk ribbon, Cream
Neutral sewing thread
Long straw needle

EMBROIDERY

FOR ALL THREE PILLOWS

STEP ONE

Fold the fabric over double so that it measures 12.5 cm x 20 cm (5 in x 8 in). Sew around three sides with a small machine stitch. To keep the corners square, stitch as shown in figure 1. Turn the piece right side out, making sure all the corners are pushed out completely.

STEP TWO

Stuff the pillow very, very firmly. When you think it is properly stuffed, use the stuffing tool to push more stuffing down the sides and into the corners. This will ensure your pillow remains firm. Close the open side with a ladder stitch.

ROSES AND LACE PILLOW

Hint: To take the whiteness out of the lace motifs, dye them in a little strawberry tea.

STEP ONE

To make the roses, tie a neat knot approximately 2.5 cm (1 in) from the end of the ribbon (Fig. 2). Holding the short end against the long end, tie off the top by winding thread around, just below the knot. This forms the centre of the rose (Fig. 3).

STEP TWO

Fold back the top edge of the ribbon and begin rolling and folding until you have a pleasing rose-like shape. With each full turn, stitch through the base to hold the rose securely (Fig. 4). When the rose is completed, cut the ribbon and secure the last roll with stitching, leaving a long thread for attaching the rose. Make at least twelve roses.

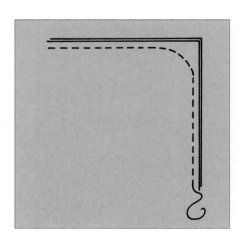

Fig. 1

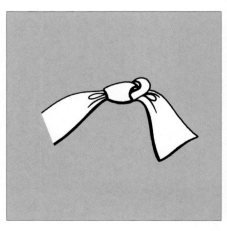

Fig. 2

STEP THREE

For the rose buds, fold the short end of a piece of Pink silk ribbon. Fold the other end over as shown in figure 5, then tie off the ribbon by winding around with thread (Fig. 6). Wrap the bud with Green ribbon and catch it securely at the base (Fig. 7). Make at least six buds in this way.

STEP FOUR

Make five leaves in the same way as the rose buds, omitting the final step.

STEP FIVE

Centre, then stitch the lace motifs onto the top of the pillow. Pin the roses, leaves and rose buds around the motifs. When you are pleased with the arrangement, sew the leaves and buds on first, then attach the roses, working from the edge to the centre.

ROSE SPRAY PILLOW

STEP ONE

Make two roses in the same way as the roses on the Roses and Lace Pillow. Arrange the leaves on the pillow, using pins to hold them in position. Place the roses amongst the leaves, then stitch the leaves to the pillow, using the sewing thread.

STEP TWO

Cut the silk ribbon in half and fold it into loops and tails. Stitch the ribbon under the roses, then stitch the roses into place. You may need to catch the petals into place with a couple of small stitches.

BUTTONS AND LACE PILLOW

STEP ONE

Cut the lace into two lengths which will fit around the pillow, following the shape of the motifs in the lace. Stitch the lace to the pillow, covering it completely and having the ends of the lace meet on the back of the pillow.

STEP TWO

Make one rose, two buds and one leaf, following the directions given for the Roses and Lace Pillow. Stitch them to the top of the pillow, using the long needle.

STEP THREE

Using the Perle thread, stitch through the buttons, tying off the thread at the back. Glue the buttons into position around the rose.

STEP FOUR

Thread the silk ribbon between the fabric of the pillow and the lace up to the side of the rose. Attach it to the rose with tiny stitches. Thread a heart, then tie a bow. Trim the ribbon ends. Attach the second heart to the other side of the rose.

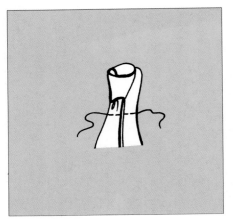

Fig. 3

Fig. 4

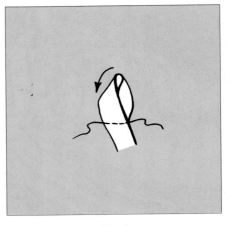

Fig. 5

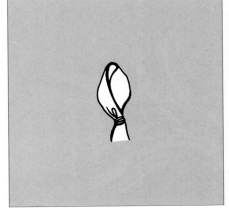

Fig. 6

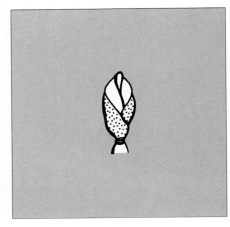

Fig. 7

TRINKET BOX

Stitched by Piecemakers Store, California

**Show off your embroidery skills to the best advantage
with this glorious trinket box.**

MATERIALS

15 cm (6 in) square of black velvet
1 m (1⅛ yd) each of 4 mm (³/₁₆ in)
    wide silk ribbon: Cream, Green
1 m (1⅛ yd) each of 7 mm (⁵/₁₆ in)
    wide silk ribbon: Purple, Mauve
1 m (1⅛ yd) each of 12 mm (½ in)
    wide overdyed silk bias ribbon:
    Green, Purple
Kanagawa silk twist thread, Green
Wooden box kit
Piecemakers chenille needle, size 22
Crewel needle, size 9
Thread to match the silk bias ribbon
Embroidery hoop

PREPARATION

See the embroidery design on
page 54.

Place the velvet in the embroidery
hoop and adjust it so the velvet is
held taut.

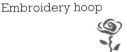

EMBROIDERY

STEP ONE

For flower 1, work the wrapped buds in
Cream silk ribbon. Begin with one
straight stitch, then wrap the ribbon
around the straight stitch twice,
keeping the ribbon lying flat (Fig. 1).
Stitch the stems in straight stitches,
using the Green silk twist.

STEP TWO

Work flower 2 in lazy daisy stitch with
French knots in the 7 mm (⁵/₁₆ in) wide
Purple ribbon. Work an open fly stitch
in the Green twist silk around the
flower and a straight stitch stem
(Fig. 2).

STEP THREE

For flower 3, work very loose French
knots in 7 mm (⁵/₁₆ in) wide Mauve
silk ribbon.

STEP FOUR

Work flower 4 as a concertina rose in
7 mm (⁵/₁₆ in) wide Purple silk ribbon in
the following way: fold approximately
15 cm (6 in) of ribbon in half at the
centre (Fig. 3). Fold the lower ribbon
to the back (Fig. 4), then fold the side
ribbon back (Fig. 5). Fold the upper
ribbon back down (Fig. 6). Continue in
this way until most of the ribbon is
used, then, holding the folded ribbons
gently in one hand, pull the lower

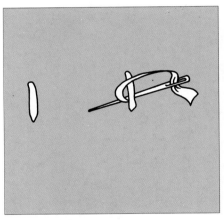

Fig. 1

Open Fly
Stitch surround
and straight
stitch stem

Fig. 2

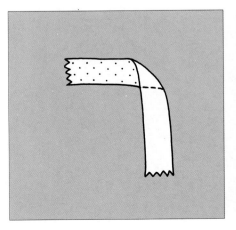

Fig. 3

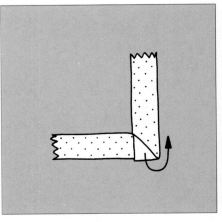

Fig. 4

ribbon through so that it forms a rose. Thread a needle with matching sewing thread and stitch backwards and forwards through the centre to hold the flower shape. Wrap the thread around the base of the flower, then cut off the excess ribbon, but do not cut the thread. Attach the flower to the velvet with the remaining thread.

Embroidery Design

STEP FIVE

Work flower 5 in the 12 mm ($^1/_2$ in) wide Purple overdyed silk bias ribbon, using approximately 45 cm (18 in) of ribbon. Thread a crewel needle with matching thread. Run a small running stitch along one edge of the ribbon, starting with a knot or several back stitches. Pull up the thread to gather the ribbon, then stitch it at the base to create the flower. Using the same thread, attach the flower to the velvet.

STEP SIX

The large leaves 6 are worked in ribbon stitch, using the Green overdyed silk bias ribbon. You can only use this in short lengths when taking it through the fabric, so each leaf is worked independently, using approximately 10 cm (4 in) of ribbon. Make four or five leaves around the major flower.

STEP SEVEN

Work the small leaves 7, using the 4 mm ($^3/_{16}$ in) wide Green silk ribbon and ribbon stitch.

MAKING UP

Make up the box according to the instructions in the box kit using the embroidered panel for the side.

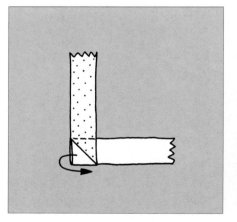

Fig. 5

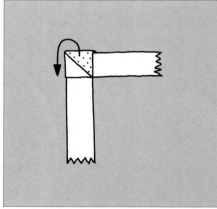

Fig. 6

CABBAGE ROSE PILLOW

Stitched by Gloria McKinnon

Lush cabbage roses are romantic and feminine and the
perfect decoration for a pillow cover. This is an ideal
project for a beginner.

MATERIALS

75 cm (30 in) of moiré fabric
50 cm (20 in) of 2.5 cm (1 in) wide
   double-sided matte ribbon,
   Deep Pink
1 m (40 in) of 2.5 cm (1 in) wide
   double-sided matte ribbon,
   Medium Pink
2 m (2¼ yd) of 2.5 cm (1 in) wide
   double-sided matte ribbon,
   Pale Pink
50 cm (20 in) of 2.5 cm (1 in) wide
   double-sided matte ribbon, Green
Sewing needle, size 8 sharp
Piecemakers tapestry needle, size 20
Embroidery hoop
Sewing thread to match the fabric
Embroidery thread, Green
30 cm (12 in) cushion insert

PREPARATION

STEP ONE

Cut two 28 cm (11 in) squares of moiré
for the pillow front and back. Cut three
strips for the ruffle, each 15 cm x
115 cm (16 in x 45 in).

STEP TWO

Place the pillow cover front in the hoop
and pull the fabric taut, then embroider
the rose, buds and leaves, following
the instructions below.

EMBROIDERY

STEP ONE

For the bud, fold down one end of the
Deep Pink ribbon at an angle of 45
degrees. Roll this end towards you
with your right hand and, at the same
time, fold and roll the rest of the ribbon
away from you with your left hand.
Stitch the base of the bud together as
you go. Use as much ribbon as you
want – the more you use, the bigger
the bud.

Hint: The method described above is
quite difficult to master but here is a
clever trick which produces a beautiful
bud. Take a 10 cm (4 in) length of
ribbon and tie a loose knot in the
centre then bring both tails of the knot

Tie a knot for the centre

Darker coloured petals around the centre

The final round of petals is a lighter colour

together underneath the knot. Tease out the loops of the knot a little to adjust the shape of the bud. Cut the tails back to approximately 1.5 cm (³/₄ in). When you stitch the bud to the pillow cover, stitch it so that the tails lie flat and the bud stands upright.

STEP TWO

For the rose, first make a bud in the way described above. Cut four 9 cm (3¹/₂ in) lengths of the Medium Pink ribbon. Fold both ends of each piece down at an angle of 45 degrees. Run a curved line of basting along the lower edge of each length, catching the folded ends in the stitching. Pull up the basting to gather the ribbon, forming petals. Stitch each petal to the base of the bud in a natural-looking way.

STEP THREE

Repeat step 2 with a group of petals in the Pale Pink ribbon. You will need six or seven petals in the second row and eight or nine petals in the third row. In the last row, make only four or five petals going just halfway around the rose so that the centre doesn't look like a bullseye.

STEP FOUR

Thread the tapestry needle with the Green ribbon. Beginning on the wrong side, bring the needle up through the fabric close to the base of the rose. Lay the ribbon flat and take a stitch of the desired length (usually approximately 1 cm (³/₈ in), reinserting the needle through the ribbon itself. This is called 'ribbon stitch' and it is this method which folds the ends of the leaves into a gentle point. When the leaves are in place, stitch lines of stem stitch in Green embroidery thread to join the leaves and flowers together.

MAKING UP

STEP ONE

Join the short ends of the ruffle strip to form a loop. Fold the loop over double with the wrong sides together. Divide the strip into quarters and mark the quarter points with pins. Gather the raw edges together and pull up the gathering to fit around the pillow front. Pin the ruffle around the pillow front, matching the pin marks to the corners. Stitch the ruffle in place.

STEP TWO

Place the front and back together with the right sides facing and the ruffle sandwiched in between. Stitch around the edge in the ruffle stitching line, leaving one side open for turning and taking care not to catch the ruffle in the stitching. Turn the cushion cover to the right side. Place the insert inside and slipstitch the opening closed.

ROSE SAMPLER

Stitched by Judy Pickett and Nelleke Clark

Two friends contributed their skill and love of embroidery
to create this beautiful heart-shaped sampler pillow.

MATERIALS

25 cm (10 in) of diamond-tucked silk
30 cm (12 in) of dupion silk for the
   ruffle and the pillow back
Sewing thread to match the fabric
Seed pearls
Nymo thread
Embroidery hoop, 20 cm (8 in)
2 m (2¹/₄ yd) each of 4 mm (³/₁₆ in)
   wide silk ribbon: Pale Pink,
   Medium Pink, Pale Green, Green
2 m (2¹/₄ yd) each of 7 mm (⁵/₁₆ in)
   wide silk ribbon: Pale Pink,
   Medium Pink, White
One skein each of stranded cotton:
   Pale Green, Grey/Green
One spool each of metallic thread:
   Green, Silver
One skein each of silk thread:
   Pale Pink, Medium Pink, White,
   Pale Green
Straw needle, size 8
Tapestry needle, size 22
Beading needle
Polyester fibre fill

PREPARATION

See the pattern/embroidery design on
page 61.

STEP ONE

Using the pattern/embroidery design,
cut out two hearts from the silk fabric,
allowing a generous seam allowance
and a strip 7 cm x 1 m (2³/₄ in x 1¹/₈ yd)
for the ruffle. Overlock the edges of the
hearts to prevent them fraying.

STEP TWO

Sew on four seed pearls at each inter-
section of the grid.

EMBROIDERY

Work the embroidery in each diamond
individually following the numbered
key. Don't feel obliged to follow exactly
the designs as given, but experiment
with your own ideas. Try different com-
binations of ribbons and threads to
achieve interesting effects. Allow some
of the embroidered flowers to trail
over the boundaries of the diamonds.
Mix techniques in the one diamond and
layer colours and stitches for added
interest. Variety is the key.

STEP ONE

For diamond 1, work French knots in
Medium Pink and Pale Pink silk thread.
Each bunch has two small ribbon stitch
leaves in Pale Green silk ribbon.

STEP TWO

For diamond 2, using the 7 mm (⁵/₁₆ in)
wide silk ribbon, work two wound roses
– one in Pale Pink, one in Medium Pink
as on page 46. For the bud, work three
bullion stitches in Medium Pink silk
thread. The leaves are three straight
stitches in Green.

STEP THREE

For diamond 3, work the trailing stem
in metallic Green thread. For the
flowers, work two straight stitches in
Medium Pink 4 mm (³/₁₆ in) ribbon,
edged with straight stitches in White
silk thread. For the buds, work straight
stitches in White silk thread with metallic Green surrounds.

STEP FOUR

For diamond 4, work a folded rose,
using the 7 mm (⁵/₁₆ in) wide Pale
Pink and White silk ribbons. For the
leaves, work looped ribbon stitch in
Pale Green.

Fig. 1

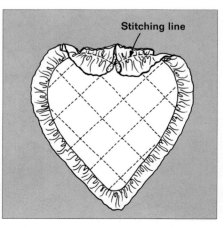

Stitching line

Fig. 2

STEP FIVE

For diamond 5, work forget-me-nots with four straight stitches with a lazy daisy stitch around each one in Pale Pink. The buds are worked in the same way.

STEP SIX

For diamond 6, work a bullion rose in Pink silk thread. Work some of the leaves in metallic Green thread and some in Green silk ribbon lazy daisy stitches.

STEP SEVEN

For diamond 7, work the rose in 7 mm ($^5/_{16}$ in) wide Pink and White silk ribbon. The buds are straight stitches in Pale Pink, surrounded by two straight stitches in Pink silk thread, then two straight stitches in Pale Green silk thread. The stems are in Green stranded cotton and metallic Green thread.

STEP EIGHT

For diamond 8, work a fly-stitch rose, using 4 mm ($^3/_{16}$ in) wide Pale Pink and Medium Pink silk ribbon. The buds are Pale Pink straight stitches with Pink silk thread French knots and Pale Green silk thread lazy daisy stitch leaves.

STEP NINE

For diamond 9, work the rosebuds as three bullion stitches with straight stitch thread and ribbon surrounds. Work the leaves and stems in Pale Green silk thread.

STEP TEN

For diamond 10, work four small Pale Pink silk thread bullion roses with Pink silk thread French knots in between and Green lazy daisy leaves.

STEP ELEVEN

For diamond 11, work a wound rose in 7 mm ($^5/_{16}$ in) wide White ribbon. The buds are straight stitches in White with bullions in White silk thread with metallic Green stems and bud surrounds.

STEP TWELVE

For diamond 12, work a rose in Medium Pink and Pale Pink, surrounded by Green silk ribbon. The leaves are Green stranded cotton mixed with metallic Green thread.

STEP THIRTEEN

For diamond 13, work the blossom in White silk thread straight stitches with Pink silk thread surrounds. The stem is Pale Green stranded cotton mixed with Silver thread.

STEP FOURTEEN

For diamond 14, work the wisteria in the same way as for diamond 1 with buds in White silk thread.

STEP FIFTEEN

Work trails of weeping blossoms across the top of diamonds 1, 2, 3 and 4 in your choice of colours and threads.

MAKING UP

STEP ONE

Fold the ruffle strip over double, with the wrong sides facing. Gather the raw edges together with two rows of gathering stitches. Pin the ruffle around the embroidered heart with the raw edges even, beginning and ending at the centre top. Fold the ends of the ruffle as indicated in figure 1. Stitch the ruffle in place in the line of the gathering and stitching the top as indicated in figure 2.

STEP TWO

Place the front and the back together with the right sides facing and the ruffle sandwiched in between. Stitch around the outside edge, leaving a 6 cm (2$^1/_2$ in) opening in one side. Turn the pillow right side out and stuff it lightly, then slipstitch the opening closed.

A variety of stitches and threads make this pretty sampler pillow

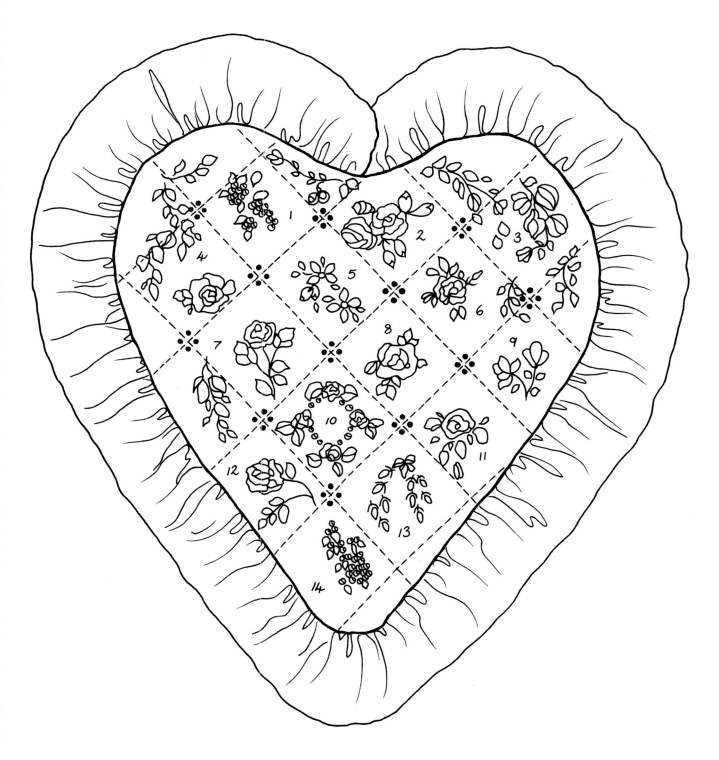

Embroidery Design

EASTER POSY

Made by Anne's Glory Box

What a pretty piece to lay over the back of your favourite chair. The combination of cosy wool and silk ribbons works so well.

MATERIALS

80 cm (32 in) of blanket wool

1 m (1⅛ yd) of 140 cm (55 in) wide or 1.4 m (1½ yd) of 115 cm (45 in) wide fabric for the backing

4.2 m (4½ yd) of 2.5 cm (1 in) wide silk ribbon, Pink

9.5 m (10½ yd) of 2.5 cm (1 in) wide silk ribbon, Pale Pink

1 m (1⅛ yd) of 2.5 cm (1 in) wide silk ribbon, Blue

5 m (5½ yd) of 4 mm (³/₁₆ in) wide silk ribbon, Yellow

Piecemakers tapestry needle, size 22

Appleton's Crewel Wool: two skeins each of Brilliant White and Pale Blue, one skein of Pale Lemon

Gossamer Mohair Wool, two skeins of Green

Water-soluble marker pen

Ordinary sewing thread to match the ribbons and the blanket wool

PREPARATION

See the embroidery design on page 65.

Using the marker pen, lightly draw the stems and leaves on the centre of the blanket wool.

EMBROIDERY

STEP ONE

Embroider the leaves and leaf stems with Green Gossamer Mohair Wool in stem stitch. For the main stems, work three rows of stem stitch very close together. Stitch the main vein on each leaf in stem stitch and the smaller veins in a single straight stitch.

STEP TWO

For the forget-me-nots, work a small straight stitch from **A** to **B** over approximately two threads of the blanket wool using one strand of Pale Blue Appleton's Wool. Work another three straight stitches from **A** to **B**, each time laying the stitch away from the centre of the flower. Stitch **B** to **C**, **C** to **D**, and **D** to **A** in the same way (Fig. 1). For the centre, work a French knot using one strand of Pale Lemon.

STEP THREE

Fill the remaining space in the entire centre of the posy with Easter daisies. These daisies are stitched using one strand of Brilliant White and working two rounds of lazy daisy stitch, following figures 2, 3 and 4. Note that the second round of lazy daisy stitches has eight shorter petals placed between the first round. For the centres, work a French knot in Yellow silk ribbon.

STEP FOUR

The roses should be placed last of all. You will need at least twelve roses, five of which should be larger than the others. Use the darker pink ribbon for the centre of the rose and the lighter pink for the outer petals. Fold over the end of the darker pink ribbon (Fig. 5). Begin rolling the ribbon around this centre. Using the matching thread, stitch through the base of the rose to secure it (Fig. 6). Continue to fold and roll the ribbon until the centre is the size you want. Turn the ribbon down and stitch it to the base.

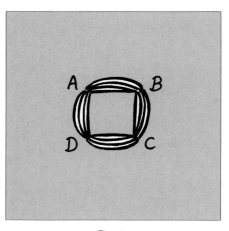

Fig. 1

Fig. 2

63

Fig. 3

Fig. 4

STEP FIVE

Fold over the end of the paler ribbon and continue to fold and roll it around the centre. Do not keep these petals too tight but allow them to stand out a little. When the rose is the desired size, cut the ribbon and stitch the end to the base, but do not cut the thread. Leave a long tail so you can use the same thread to attach the rose to the blanket wool.

MAKING UP

STEP ONE

Lay the backing fabric face down on a hard surface. Centre the embroidered blanket wool, face upwards, on top. There should be a 10 cm (4 in) border of the backing fabric showing all around. Baste the blanket wool to the backing horizontally, vertically and diagonally through the corners.

STEP TWO

Fold the backing fabric to meet the edge of the blanket wool, then fold it again so the folded edge is over the edge of the blanket wool. Pin the folded edge in place, mitring the corners. Slipstitch the backing to the blanket wool, but take care not to stitch through to the back. Stitch the mitres.

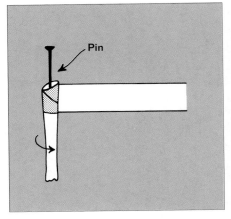

Fig. 5

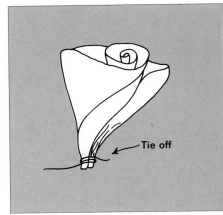

Fig. 6

Silk roses make a charming feature on this wool blanket

Rose placement

Blue forget-me-not areas

Leaves and stems - stem stitch

Embroider Stems - 3 rows stem stitch

Embroidery Design

65

ROSE SHOES AND PURSE

Stitched by Margaret B. Woolfe

This delightful set of evening shoes and matching bag is quite simple to make when you have mastered the basic rose. All the roses are made in exactly the same way. The apparent variety is provided by the use of ribbons of different textures, widths and colours.

MATERIALS

Pump-style fabric-covered shoes
Purse, either purchased or
   handmade
Variety of ribbons including silk,
   velvet, metallic and French
   wired ribbon
E6000 glue
Sewing needle
Sewing threads to match the ribbons
Chenille needle or tapestry needle
Hat pin or toothpick
Fine wire or Bouillion
Corrugated cardboard or styrofoam
Plastic wrap
Crinoline

MAKING ROSES

STEP ONE

For each rose bud, you will need seven times the width of the ribbon you are using. Beginning close to one end of the ribbon, fold down the end diagonally (Fig. 1). Fold the width of the ribbon in half again, folding diagonally (Fig. 2). And again (Fig. 3).

STEP TWO

Insert the hat pin or toothpick into the folds and roll the ribbon up around the pin or toothpick to form the centre of the rose bud. Remove the pin, but keep a firm hold with your thumb and index finger to prevent the ribbon unrolling

again (Fig. 4). Fold the loose part of the ribbon away from you, again folding on the diagonal. Still holding the base with your thumb and index finger, roll in the direction indicated by the arrow (Fig. 5). In order to roll the base of the rose bud along the inner edge of the ribbon, you will automatically force the folded edge of the ribbon to remain at the top of the rose bud and flare out just slightly. When you have 'used up' the folded edge, fold the ribbon away from you again, just as you did the first time. Continue to fold and roll in this way until you have used all the ribbon, leaving a tail approximately 2.5 cm (1 in) long.

STEP THREE

Sew a row of gathering stitches across the tail end of the ribbon (Fig. 6). Remove the needle but do not cut the thread. Draw up the gathering, then secure the end to the base of the rose bud with a few stitches. Wrap the thread several times around the base of the rose bud, then secure it with a knot (Fig. 7).

STEP FOUR

The full-bloom rose is best worked with wired ribbon. You will need a length that is twelve to fourteen times the width of the ribbon. Every fold you make will stay in place if you crimp the wire slightly. Begin by following steps one to five for the rose bud to make a centre for the rose. Secure the base of the centre with a few stitches, then cut the thread.

STEP FIVE

Carefully remove the wire from the bottom edge of the remaining ribbon. Gather the bottom edge (Fig. 8). Loosely wrap the gathering around the base. Pinch in the loose end and secure it in place with some wire or with a few stitches. Flatten the rose with your hand or, very gently, with a steam iron. Arrange the 'petals' attractively, crimping and pinching the wired edge to create a pleasing shape.

STEP SIX

For the leaf, use a length of wired ribbon, seven to ten times the width of the ribbon. Carefully pull out 12 mm ($^1/_2$ in) of the wire from the same side of both cut ends of the ribbon. Gripping these ends of wire between your thumb and index finger, continue working the ribbon onto the wire until it is fully gathered (Fig. 9). Pinch the cut ends together and wind the wire around to form the stem (Fig. 10). To close the centre 'seam' of the leaf, apply a small amount of glue and press the edges together for a few seconds.

STEP SEVEN

For the loop rosette, use 30-35 cm (12-14 in) of 3 mm ($^1/_8$ in) metallic or silk ribbon. Using matching thread and a needle, take small stitches along the ribbon at approximately 2.5-4 cm (1-1$^1/_2$ in) intervals, beginning and ending approximately 2.5 cm (1 in) from the end of the ribbon (Fig. 11). Pull up the thread to form the rosette. Secure the thread with a lock stitch (Fig. 12).

Make vines by coiling fine wire tightly onto a toothpick or chenille or tapestry needle. Remove the toothpick or needle, then pull the coil slightly to extend it. There is available a very tightly coiled super-fine wire material, called Bouillion, which is ideal. This delightful stuff comes in copper, silver and gold.

STEP NINE

For the flat bud or leaf, fold one end of a length of ribbon four times its width (Fig. 13). Cross-fold the ribbon and gather as shown in figure 14. Pull up the thread tightly, then wrap the thread around the ends of the ribbon to form a stem (Fig. 15).

MAKING UP

STEP ONE

Cover a 25 cm (10 in) square of corrugated cardboard or styrofoam with plastic wrap. This will be your work surface. Arrange your composition of roses, leaves, rosettes and vines on a piece of crinoline that is approximately the size of the shoe front or the purse flap. Remember to use black crinoline for dark colours and white crinoline for pastels. Any excess crinoline can be cut away from the back when the whole arrangement of flowers is assembled and secure.

Place the piece of crinoline on the work space. Begin by placing the leaves and flat buds. Next, place your focal flower, usually the largest rose. Add in the smaller roses, rose buds, leaves, loop rosettes and vines. These filler pieces can be tucked into empty spaces or be peeping out from behind a larger flower. When you are pleased with your arrangement, glue it into place on the crinoline. Trim the crinoline from the back, then glue it into place on the shoes and the purse.

If you wish to know more about this craft, read *Small Treasures in Victorian Ribbonwork* by Margaret B. Woolfe.

Transform a simple bag into a romantic evening accessory

68

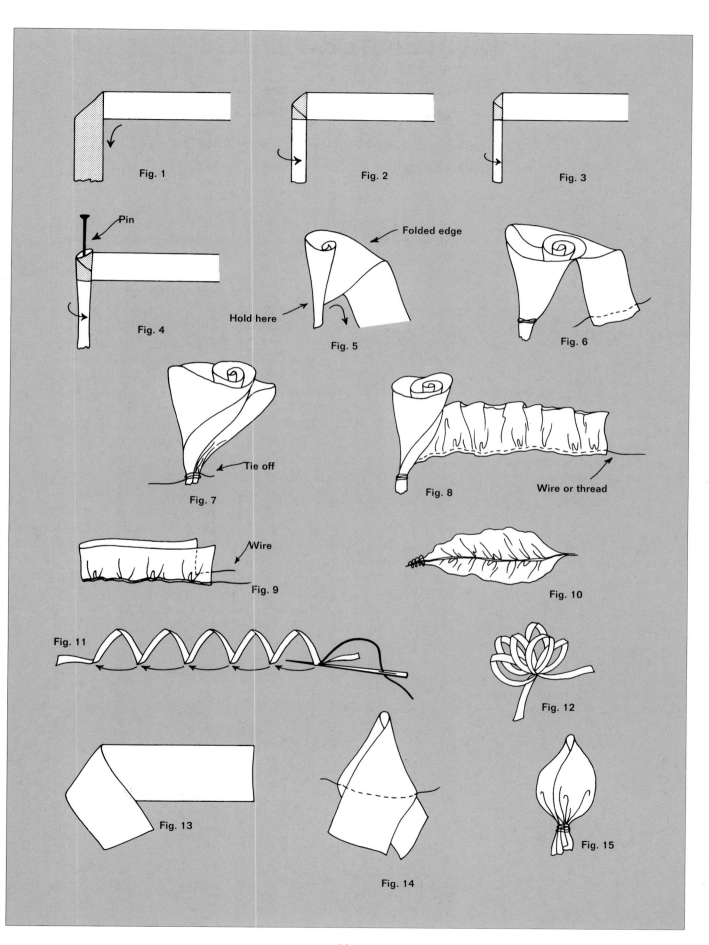

Fig. 1

Fig. 2

Fig. 3

Pin

Fig. 4

Folded edge

Hold here

Fig. 5

Fig. 6

Tie off

Fig. 7

Wire or thread

Fig. 8

Wire

Fig. 9

Fig. 10

Fig. 11

Fig. 12

Fig. 13

Fig. 14

Fig. 15

BATTENBERG DUET

Made by Kathy Awender

Inexpensive purchased Battenberg pieces form the basis for this delightful tea cosy and table runner set.

MATERIALS

Two Battenberg lace table runners
50 cm (20 in) of lawn for lining the
   tea cosy
3 m (3¹/₄ yd) each of 4 mm (³/₁₆ in)
   wide silk ribbon: Pale Blue, Pale
   Pink, Mid-pink, Lemon, Pale Lilac,
   Green, Butter Yellow
DMC Stranded Cotton: Lemon, Pale
   Green, Pale Blue
Piecemakers tapestry needle, size 22
Piecemakers crewel needle, size 8
30 cm (12 in) of low-loft wadding
Water-soluble marker pen

EMBROIDERY

See the embroidery design and the pattern on page 72.

STEP ONE

Transfer the embroidery design to both ends of one table runner and only one end of the second table runner. The simplest way to do this is to place a small dot with the marker pen at the position of each major flower.

STEP TWO

Embroider the flowers, following the embroidery design and the key.

STEP THREE

For the bow, fit the Pale Blue silk ribbon around the flowers in a pleasing bow shape. Secure the loops of the bow with French knots worked in two strands of Pale Blue cotton. Leave the tails of the bow quite loose, stitching through the fabric at intervals, leaving a space for French knots as for the loops.

TEA COSY

STEP ONE

Using the pattern provided, cut out the front of the tea cosy from the embroidered end of the table runner and the back from a plain section. Using the same pattern, cut two pieces of wadding and three lining pieces.

STEP TWO

Lay the embroidered piece over one lining piece, matching the notches. Baste them together and, from here on, treat them as a single piece.

STEP THREE

Baste a wadding piece to the back of the Battenberg/lining piece and to the back of the plain piece. With the right sides facing and the raw edges even, stitch a lining piece to the front and back pieces along the straight edge. Open each section out as shown in figure 1.

STEP FOUR

Pin the two pieces together with the right sides facing and the outer sections together. Stitch around the outside edge, leaving an opening between the notches on the lining. Turn the tea cosy to the right side. Slipstitch the opening closed. Push the lining into the tea cosy.

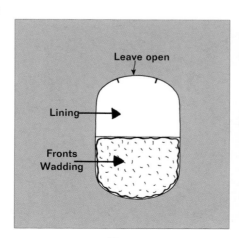

Fig. 1

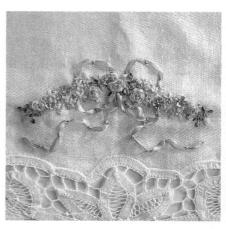

Pretty flowers work well with crisp lace

Cups, Spectacles from Mosman Antique Centre, NSW

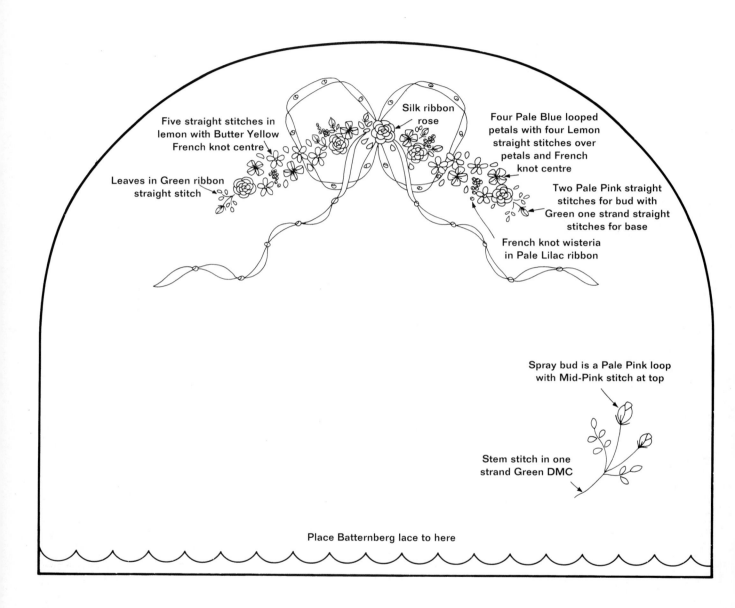

Five straight stitches in lemon with Butter Yellow French knot centre

Silk ribbon rose

Four Pale Blue looped petals with four Lemon straight stitches over petals and French knot centre

Leaves in Green ribbon straight stitch

Two Pale Pink straight stitches for bud with Green one strand straight stitches for base

French knot wisteria in Pale Lilac ribbon

Spray bud is a Pale Pink loop with Mid-Pink stitch at top

Stem stitch in one strand Green DMC

Place Batternberg lace to here

Tea Cosy Pattern and Embroidery Design

Please note: This pattern has been reduced.
The actual size is 25 cm x 30 cm (10 in x 12 in).

WATERLILY PIN CUSHION

Stitched by Mariko O'Hara

Make this pretty little pin cushion to hold your
special brooches and hatpins.

MATERIALS

Petals, 7 mm (5/16 in) wide silk ribbon
    pack in chosen waterlily colours
2 m (2¼ yd) each of 4 mm (3/16 in)
    wide silk ribbon: Blue, Cream
1 m (1⅛ yd) each of 4 mm (3/16 in)
    wide silk ribbon: Yellow, Green,
    Old Gold
2 m (2¼ yd) of 7 mm (5/16 in) wide
    silk ribbon, Green
Round cardboard box kit
30 cm (12 in) of moiré fabric
30 cm (12 in) of cotton velveteen
50 cm (20 in) of cord trim to match
    the moiré
30 cm (12 in) of Pellon
Cotton thread to match the moiré
Piecemakers tapestry needle, size 24
Small embroidery hoop
Craft glue
Polyester fibre fill
Ordinary sewing thread, Black

PREPARATION

See the embroidery design on
page 74.

STEP ONE

Cut a length of moiré big enough to
cover the long strip of cardboard in the
box kit for the box side. Make sure the
fabric is at least 12 mm (½ in) larger all
around than the cardboard. Cut a
piece of Pellon to the same size.

STEP TWO

Sew a line of basting stitches 5 cm (2 in)
from the bottom edge of the fabric. This
line is a guide for your embroidery
and will sit 12 mm (½ in) above the
pincushion base.

STEP THREE

Secure the fabric in the embroidery
hoop and make sure it is held taut.

EMBROIDERY

STEP ONE

Embroider the waterlilies first. Stitch
the stems in stem stitch, using the 7 mm
(5/16 in) wide Green ribbon and twisting
the ribbon so the stem is fine.

STEP TWO

Using ribbon stitch, make three leaves
for each flower and two leaves for
each stem, using the 7 mm (5/16 in) wide
Green ribbon.

STEP THREE

Using the 7 mm (5/16 in) wide ribbon
in your chosen flower colours, make
four ribbon stitches for the petals
(Fig. 1). The centre of the flower is a
lazy daisy stitch with a two-wrap
bullion tip (Figs 2 and 3).

Embroidery Design

STEP FOUR

For the four pistil stitches, bring the needle to the front at the flower centre. Twist the ribbon, then complete the stitch with a small French knot just beyond the ends of the petals.

STEP FIVE

For the base of the waterlilies, make five ribbon stitches (Fig. 4).

STEP SIX

Using the Cream ribbon, stitch a daisy with five petals. Work a French knot in the centre, using the Old Gold ribbon, then with the 4 mm ($^3/_{16}$ in) wide Green ribbon, stitch ribbon stitch leaves.

STEP SEVEN

For the forget-me-nots, begin with a Yellow French knot centre, then stitch five tight French knots in Blue, evenly around the centre. Use the forget-me-nots to fill any gaps in the embroidery.

MAKING UP

STEP ONE

When the embroidery is completed, baste the fabric and the Pellon together. Make up the box according to the instructions in the kit. Glue the cord trim around the base of the box.

STEP TWO

From the velveteen, cut a 22 cm (8½ in) diameter circle. Sew running stitches around the edge, then pull up the thread to gather the circle into a ball. Fill the ball very firmly with the fibre fill, then pull the thread very tightly to close the base and form a ball. Tie off the threads. Glue the ball into the box, taking care to keep the edges of the velvet as smooth as possible.

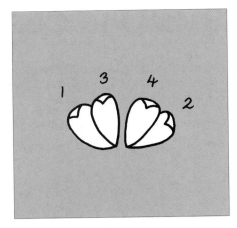

Fig. 1

Fig. 2

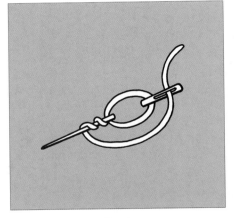

Fig. 3

Fig. 4

SUNFLOWER PICTURE

Stitched by Gloria McKinnon

Awash with bright yellow sunflowers, this little picture will add warmth and cheer to any room.

MATERIALS

Two pieces of yellow fabric, each
  30 cm x 40 cm (12 in x 16 in)
30 cm x 40 cm (12 in x 16 in) of
  Rayfelt
40 cm (8 in) of fabric for the mat
  (optional)
10 m (11 yd) of 4 mm ($^3/_{16}$ in) wide
  silk ribbon, Golden Yellow
10 m (11 yd) each of 4 mm ($^3/_{16}$ in)
  wide silk ribbon: Brown, Reddish
  Brown
10 m (11 yd) of 7 mm ($^5/_{16}$ in) wide
  overdyed silk ribbon, Yellow
5 m (5 yd) of 7 mm ($^5/_{16}$ in) wide
  ribbon, Green
Embroidery hoop, 15 cm (6 in)
Piecemakers tapestry needle, size 22
Water-soluble marker pen
Ordinary sewing thread

PREPARATION

STEP ONE

Baste together a piece of the yellow fabric and the piece of Rayfelt, working from the centre out to the corners. Finally baste the edges.

STEP TWO

On the back of the Rayfelt, mark the rectangle the flowers are to fill and run a line of stitches around the marking to transfer the shape to the front.

EMBROIDERY

STEP ONE

Place the fabric into the hoop and make it taut.

STEP TWO

Work some of the sunflowers in lazy daisy stitch using the 4 mm ($^3/_{16}$ in) wide Golden Yellow ribbon and some of the sunflowers in lazy daisy stitch using the 7 mm ($^5/_{16}$ in) overdyed Yellow ribbon. Begin each sunflower by placing the first four stitches as shown (Fig. 1). Fill in the other twelve stitches as shown in figure 2.

STEP THREE

Fill the centre area with fifteen to twenty French knots in the Brown and Reddish Brown ribbon.

STEP FOUR

Place leaves worked in Green ribbon stitch into the spaces between the sunflowers as required.

MAKING UP

Have your embroidery professionally framed. Choose a coloured mat to complement the colours in the embroidery.

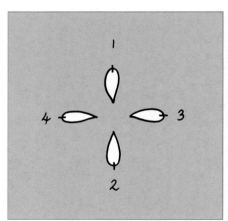

Fig. 1

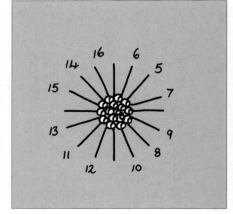

Fig. 2

IN MY GARDEN

Stitched by Kathy Awender

**This little dress uses silk ribbon flowers to create
a very special dress from a basic pattern.**

MATERIALS

Yoked dress or pinafore pattern of
your choice
Sufficient fabric to make your chosen
garment
Sufficient lawn interfacing for the
yokes
Piecemakers tapestry needle, size 22
Piecemakers crewel needle, size 8
Three ceramic garden buttons
Embroidery hoop
1 m (1¹⁄₈ yd) each of 4 mm (³⁄₁₆ in)
wide silk ribbon: Light Brown, two
shades of Purple
3.5 m (3³⁄₄ yd) of 4 mm (³⁄₁₆ in) wide
silk ribbon, Yellow

2 m (2¹⁄₄ yd) each of 4 mm (³⁄₁₆ in)
wide ribbon: Pale Lemon, Peach,
Green, two shades of Pink
4 m (4¹⁄₂ yd) of 4 mm (³⁄₁₆ in) wide
silk ribbon, Grey/Green
Kanagawa silk twist thread, Green

PREPARATION

See the embroidery designs on
page 80.

Mark the front yoke pattern onto
a piece of the fabric and cut it out
roughly in a square so it can be se-
cured in the hoop. Cut a similar square
from the lawn interfacing and baste
the two together securely.

EMBROIDERY

Complete the silk ribbon embroidery
on the front yoke, following the stitch
guide on page 80, ensuring that the
work is centred and at least 12 mm
(¹⁄₂ in) above the waist seam line.

MAKING UP

When the embroidery is completed,
attach the buttons, then complete
the garment, following the directions
provided with the pattern.

A colourful garden blooms on this pretty dress

STITCH GUIDE

TULIPS

Stems are straight stitch in Green Kanagawa silk twist thread.

Leaves are ribbon stitch in Grey/Green silk ribbon.

Petals are two ribbon stitches using two shades of Pink ribbon in the needle at once, light on top and dark underneath. Work a third petal over the top of the other two. You can reverse the colours for some flowers.

DAFFODILS

Petals are worked in the following steps:

two straight stitches in a Pale Lemon silk ribbon.

two more Pale Lemon straight stitches over the centre.

one straight stitch in Pale Lemon over the centre.

For the trumpet, work one ribbon stitch in Yellow silk ribbon.

Stems are straight stitch in Green Kanagawa silk twist thread.

Leaves are straight stitch in Green silk ribbon with the ribbon twisted.

VIOLETS

For the petals, work five small straight stitches in Purple silk ribbon with a Yellow French knot in the centre.

Large leaves are buttonhole stitch and the small leaves are ribbon stitch, both in Grey/Green silk ribbon.